ISO 9000: 2000
An A–Z Guide

ISO 9000: 2000
An A–Z Guide

David Hoyle

OXFORD AMSTERDAM BOSTON LONDON NEW YORK PARIS
SAN DIEGO SAN FRANCISCO SINGAPORE SYDNEY TOKYO

Butterworth-Heinemann
An imprint of Elsevier Science
Linacre House, Jordan Hill, Oxford OX2 8DP
225 Wildwood Avenue, Woburn, MA 01801-2041

First published 2003

British Library Cataloguing in Publication Data
A catalogue record for this book is available from the British Library

Library of Congress Cataloguing in Publication Data
A catalogue record for this book is available from the Library of Congress

ISBN 0 7506 5844 4

For information on all Butterworth-Heinemann publications visit our website at:
www.bh.com

Composition by Genesis Typesetting, Rochester, Kent
Printed and bound in Great Britain by Biddles Ltd *www.biddles.co.uk*

Contents

About the author

David Hoyle has over 30 years experience in quality management. He is currently a Director of Transition Support Ltd, a company that provides consulting, training and publications on business improvement. He has held managerial positions with British Aerospace and Ferranti International and as a management consultant, firstly with Neville-Clarke Ltd and latterly as an independent, he has guided such companies as National Semiconductors, General Motors, Civil Aviation Authority and Bell Atlantic through their ISO 9000 programmes. He has delivered quality management and auditor training courses throughout the world and published several books through Butterworth-Heinemann. His books have been translated into Spanish, Japanese, Mandarin, Italian and Korean. He is involved with various committees of the Institute of Quality Assurance and has been engaged in the year 2000 revision of ISO 9000. He is a Chartered Engineer, Fellow of the Institute of Quality Assurance and Member of the Royal Aeronautical Society. He lives in South Wales with his wife Angela and when not at his computer or with clients, likes to spend his spare time at the piano, or studying history and exploring the countryside near his home.

Preface

The changes to ISO 9000 family of International Standards reflected in the 2000 version were so significant that the approach taken with *The ISO 9000 Pocket Guide*, published in 1998, seemed no longer appropriate. The Pocket Guide was in five parts and provided both an interpretation of the requirements, and examples of how to develop and audit a quality management system. However, it resulted in a book that was too big for a pocket and was bulky in a briefcase. It also appeared to support the clause approach to the implementation of ISO 9000 when what was now needed was a more holistic approach that used ISO 9000 as a validation tool, not an implementation tool. I found that I could easily condense the requirements into one page and describe how these requirements could be met in five pages (see 'ISO 9000 in a nutshell' section), but it was difficult to find a middle way between five pages and the 600 or so pages of my *ISO 9000:2000 Quality Systems Handbook*.

The solution seemed to be an A–Z of ISO 9000:2000 that provided the flexibility to add or omit topics without the constraint of addressing all requirements. Even though the *Quality System Handbook* set out to address all requirements, I received correspondence from people pointing out that some requirements had been omitted. Grateful for the observations, I posted the missing text on our web site (http://www.transition-support.com/handbook_amendments.htm).

I searched the family of standards and chose terms that I felt warranted explanation. Where the term is used within a requirement or recommendation, I have quoted the relevant clause. This also consolidates most references in one place, thereby providing the reader with the ability to answer the question 'Where does it say that?'. Sometimes a requirement or recommendation occurs many times and, in such cases, I have been selective to avoid repetition. By way of examples showing how specific requirements can be implemented, I have included in most cases a subsection that provides application guidance.

Not all terms included in this book are used in the family of standards but they do relate to the solutions that meet the requirements. This results in there being no subsection on clauses of the standard or application guidance in some cases. In order to avoid duplication, I have cross-referenced terms using bold type to indicate terms that are explained elsewhere in the book. The CD-ROM provided with this book provides the added benefit of being able to click a term, read the explanation and return using the back button of the browser. You will require Acrobat Reader to use the CD-ROM, this is available to download free from www.adobe.com.

I have attempted to provide a companion that will help the manager or quality professional on the move. I hope it fulfils this need.

David Hoyle
Monmouth
March 2002
hoyle@transition-support.com

ISO 9000 in a nutshell

ISO 9000:2000 is fundamentally different to ISO 9000:1994. ISO 9000:1994 focuses on specific requirements born out of situations that experience had shown led to poor product quality. ISO 9000:2000 focuses on eight **quality management principles**, which, if applied effectively, lead to the satisfaction of all interested parties. This is a fundamental change from preventing failure to causing success.

- ISO 9000:2000 explains the concepts and principles, and defines the terms.
- ISO 9001:2000 specifies requirements for assessing the capability of organizations to meet customer requirements and applicable regulatory requirements – it is not a design specification for a quality management system. Also ISO 9001 is applied – it is not implemented simply because it contains assessment criteria and not design criteria. It is for this reason that systems designed around ISO 9001:1994 were not effective.
- ISO 9004:2000 contains guidance on performance improvement – it is not a guide to ISO 9001, neither is it a design specification, although it comes much closer than ISO 9001.

It is essential that users read all three standards – for without an understanding of the concepts and the terms, ISO 9001 could easily be misinterpreted. It is also important that the requirements of ISO 9001 are not taken in isolation. It is not a task list. It is intended to be applied to an operating system in which there is an infrastructure that causes the right things to happen. Many requirements are duplicated in different clauses and this is illustrated in this book.

The 250 or so requirements of ISO 9001 can be condensed into five linked requirements. ISO 9001 basically requires the organization to:

1 Determine the **needs** and **expectations** of **customers** and other **interested parties**.
2 Establish **policies**, **objectives** and a **work environment** necessary to motivate the organization to satisfy these needs.
3 Design, resource and manage a system of interconnected **processes** necessary to implement the policy and attain the objectives.
4 Measure and analyse the adequacy, efficiency and effectiveness of each process in fulfilling its purpose and objectives.
5 Pursue the **continual improvement** of the system from an objective evaluation of its performance.

The focus is, therefore, on results and the processes that produce these results. This means that there needs to be a linkage between the needs of the interested parties, the organization's objectives, the processes for achieving these objectives and the results being produced.

The old method of documenting what you do and doing what you document will not cause the right things to happen. The old method of auditing for conformity to requirements or procedures will not verify that processes are being managed effectively and, therefore, both have to change.

Also the idea that an effective system can be created simply by addressing the requirements of ISO 9001 through documented procedures is flawed. It creates a *bolt-on system* that sits outside the business, whereas to deliver customer satisfaction, it requires the processes to be an integral part of the organization.

So how might such a system be developed and do we have to throw away our existing system of documentation? To begin with, a number of perceptions need to change. It requires the system to be perceived as shown in Figure 1 and not as shown in Figure 2.

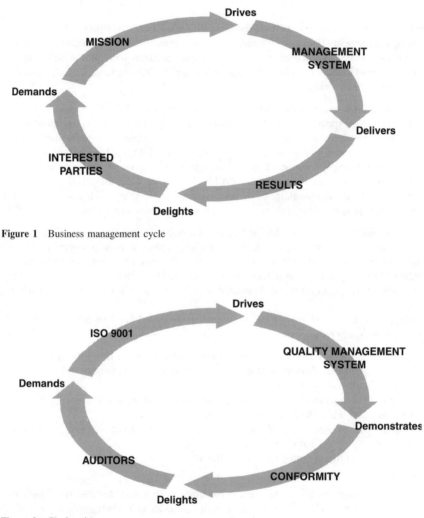

Figure 1   Business management cycle

Figure 2   Conformity

Organizations have only one system. It is a dynamic system, not simply a set of procedures – it comprises all the processes needed to achieve the organization's objectives.

ISO 9001 simply focuses on those aspects of this business management system that serve to deliver customer satisfaction. Other standards focus on environmental, security, or health and safety aspects of this system. It is not intended that the organization somehow create entirely separate systems. People do not do a job then apply quality, environmental, security and safety measures. They do all these things when doing the job so that the job is done in a way that results in satisfying customers, protecting the environment, securing information, and preserving health and safety of individuals.

Quality manuals based on the elements of the standard are no longer appropriate. What is needed is a system description showing how the needs and expectations of the organization's interested parties are satisfied – how objectives are established, how processes are developed and managed, and how performance is measured and improved.

Processes convert inputs into outputs but what is required are managed processes, and these consolidate the resources, activities and behaviours needed to achieve specified objectives – objectives derived from the needs of interested parties, not the requirements of the standard.

Procedures will still be required but are task-focused, not results-focused. Not only is each organization different, the knowledge, skills and perceptions of those whose task it is to create or convert an effective management system are also different. It is, therefore, difficult to lay out a simple solution. What follows is a sequence of events that will be typical of an organization that wishes to embrace the intent of ISO 9000:2000.

1 Determine how the quality management system is perceived within the organization, why it exists, what it does, what it doesn't do, what it should do.
2 Develop a clear understanding of the **intent of the standard** – what it sets out to do and the principles than underpin the requirements.
3 Use facilitated sessions to produce and test understanding of the terminology used in the standard and how perceptions differ – e.g. **system, process, process management, procedure, policies, objectives, audit, system effectiveness** and **continual improvement**.
4 Cause management to separate in their mind ISO 9000, ISO 9000 certification and the quality management system such that they are no longer inseparable but three independent concepts.
5 Cause management to perceive the organization as a system that enables achievement of their goals and to think of this system as the **Business Management System**.
6 Determine the size of the gap between where the organization thinks it is and where it needs to be to have an effective business management system.
7 Establish whether there is a customer specific requirement for ISO 9000 **certification**.
8 Debate at top management level the merits of **ISO 9000** certification and agree that independent of whether or not certification is a customer requirement it does not change their resolve to develop an effective business management system.
9 Get agreement to commencing the conversion.
10 Determine or clarify the **mission** of the organization.
11 Identify the **factors that affect the ability of the organization to fulfil its mission**.
12 For each factor define the objectives that need to be achieved, the measures of success and performance targets.
13 For the objectives, **identify the processes** needed for their achievement.
14 Train managers in the **process approach** to the management of work.
15 For each process define the inputs required.
16 For each process define the key stages that convert the inputs into outputs.
17 For each stage in each process define the **resources**, information and **competencies** required to deliver the required outputs.
18 For each stage in each process define the stage outputs and the means by which the outputs will be verified.

19 For each stage in each process identify the risks and their impacts. Put in place measures that eliminate, reduce or **control** these risks.

20 For each process determine how performance will be measured against the objectives and **variation** reduced.

21 For each process establish how process efficiency will be determined and improved.

22 For each process establish how process effectiveness will be determined and policies and objectives changed.

23 Communicate the changes to and involve all those affected.

24 Implement the **process approach**.

25 Measure the performance of each process.

26 Establish a timetable for the review of performance.

27 Evaluate organizational performance against the declared objectives.

28 Undertake improvements in performance to meet targets.

29 Review targets and objectives periodically and initiate changes to ensure the organization's objectives are aligned to the needs and expectations of all the interested parties.

It was stated previously that requirements should not taken in isolation. It is through linking requirements that a clear picture emerges of what the standard is about. The figure puts this in perspective, showing how the important requirements are linked together.

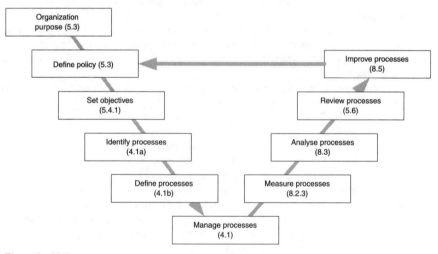

Figure 3   V diagram

Acceptance criteria

Meaning

Acceptance criteria are the standards against which a comparison is made to judge conformance.

ISO 9000 requirements and recommendations

- Clause 7.3.3 of ISO 9001 – design and development outputs are required to contain or reference product acceptance criteria.
- Clause 8.2.4 of ISO 9001 – requires evidence of conformity with the acceptance criteria to be maintained.

Application

Acceptance criteria are often expressed in documents such as standards, specifications and drawings, in pictures or in the form of samples showing acceptable and unacceptable characteristics. The documents, pictures and samples should be **controlled** so as to prevent unauthorized change once they have been approved for use.

Accreditation

Meaning

Accreditation is a process by which organizations are authorized to conduct certification of conformity to prescribed standards. Organizations may be accredited for certifying product, personnel or management systems. The standards used in Europe that organizations need to meet in order to become accredited are as follows:

- EN 45011: General criteria for certification bodies operating product certification.
- EN 45012: General criteria for certification bodies operating quality management system certification.
- EN 45013: General criteria for certification bodies operating certification of personnel.

The term 'accreditation' is sometimes used when in fact what is meant is 'certification'. Organizations seek **certification** to ISO 9001, for instance, whereas the bodies that certify them would seek accreditation to EN 45012.

ISO 9000 requirements and recommendations

There are no requirements or recommendations in ISO 9000 for accreditation.

Application

If you require confidence that the products, personnel or systems you are using conform to specified standards, you can verify the products, personnel or system yourself, or engage the services of a third party to provide independent certification. Self-certified products, personnel and systems may be satisfactory, but have the disadvantage that the certification is not recognized by other organizations or nations (they cannot be certain of its integrity). In order to provide confidence that the results reported by third parties are of the highest integrity, you would select those that have been accredited by an organization with international recognition to certify the types of products, personnel and systems that you intend to use.

Accreditation body

Meaning

An accreditation body is an organization that accredits other organizations to conduct certification of conformity.

ISO 9000 requirements and recommendations

ISO 9000 does not address accreditation bodies.

Application

Accreditation is granted by accreditation bodies (ABs), such as the United Kingdom Accreditation Service (UKAS), the Registrar Accreditation Board (RAB), the Raad voor Accreditatie (RvA) and the Swedish Board for Accreditation and Conformity Assessment (SWEDAC), and is normally recognized by the national government. These ABs have formed an alliance in the International Accreditation Forum (IAF), where they have signed agreements giving mutual recognition to each other's accreditation standards. For example, UKAS-accredited organizations are accepted by RAB as being of equal integrity as those accredited by RAB. This negates **certification bodies** having to gain multiple accreditations for the same products, personnel or systems. Other ABs exist that are not formally recognized but which nevertheless provide a bone fide accreditation service.

You would use accredited calibration laboratories as an acceptable means of demonstrating the integrity of measuring devices, or accredited certification bodies as an acceptable means of demonstrating the capability of a supplier's management system. If your products are designed to meet certain standards, you would use accredited test laboratories to certify that the products meet these standards, thus testifying their integrity to your customers.

Adequacy

Meaning

Adequacy means suitable or sufficient for the intended purpose or need.

ISO 9000 requirements and recommendations

- Clause 4.2.3 of ISO 9001 – a documented procedure is required to be established to define the controls needed to approve documents for adequacy prior to issue.
- Clause 5.6.1 of ISO 9001 – top management is required to review the organization's quality management system, at planned intervals, to ensure its continuing suitability, adequacy and effectiveness.

- Clause 7.3.2 of ISO 9001 – design inputs are required to be reviewed for adequacy.
- Clause 7.4.2 of ISO 9001 – the organization is required to ensure the adequacy of specified purchase requirements prior to their communication to the supplier.

In all the above, the subject is required to be adequate and, therefore, fit for its intended purpose. Clearly there should be nothing that is *unfit* for its intended purpose but these topics (documents, the system, design inputs and purchasing data) have been selected as of particular importance.

Application

Ensuring the adequacy of something can be accomplished by **competent** personnel using acceptance criteria. These criteria would define the intended purpose and the factors that are critical to fulfilling this purpose. For example, a competent designer would review the design inputs against a checklist or other criteria, to ensure nothing was missing and that which was present was satisfactory.

Analysis of data

Meaning

Analysis of data means extracting factual information from data for use in decision-making. This is expressed by the **factual approach** principle of quality management.

ISO 9000 requirements and recommendations

- Clause 8.1 of ISO 9001 – the organization is required to plan and implement the analysis processes to:
  (a) **demonstrate** conformity of the product;
  (b) ensure conformity of the quality management system;
  (c) continually improve the **effectiveness of the quality management system**.
- Clause 8.4 of ISO 9001 – the organization is required to:
  (a) determine, collect and analyse appropriate data to demonstrate the suitability and effectiveness of the quality management system;
  (b) determine, collect and analyse appropriate data to evaluate where continual improvement of the effectiveness of the quality management system can be made.
- Clause 8.4 of ISO 9001 – the analysis of data is required to provide information relating to:
  (a) customer satisfaction;
  (b) conformance to product requirements;
  (c) characteristics and trends of processes and products, including opportunities for preventive action;
  (d) suppliers.
- Clause 8.5.1 of ISO 9001 – the organization is required to improve the effectiveness of the quality management system continually through the use of the analysis of data.

Application

In order to analyse data, you must first of all make arrangements for the right kind of data to be collected. Your analysis will only be as good as the data with which you are provided. You also need to take care to avoid the garbage in/garbage out syndrome.

There are three important rules you need to observe:

1 Analyse data for a purpose that is relevant to the organization's performance.
2 Provide solutions to real problems – in other words confirm the existence of a problem or potential problem before action.
3 Implement those solutions that will improve performance.

Data analysis may involve any or all of the following actions:

- Devise a method for synthesizing the data for analysis.
- Use suitable presentation techniques to draw attention to the results.
- Establish the records to be created and maintained.
- Identify the reports to be issued and to whom they should be issued.
- Determine the actions and decisions to be taken and those responsible for the actions and decisions.

Applicable

Meaning

In the context of documents, applicable means capable of being applied to the activities to be undertaken. In the context of activities, applicable means where it applies.

ISO 9000 requirements and recommendations

- Clause 1.1 of ISO 9001 states that the Standard specifies requirements for a quality management system where an organization needs to demonstrate its ability to provide product that consistently meets customer and applicable regulatory requirements.
- Clause 1.2 of ISO 9001 states that all requirements of the Standard are generic and are intended to be applicable to all organizations, regardless of type, size and product provided.
- Clause 4.2.3 of ISO 9001 requires relevant versions of applicable documents to be available at points of use.
- Clause 7.3.2 of ISO 9001 requires design inputs to include applicable statutory and regulatory requirements.
- Clause 8.1 of ISO 9001 requires the planning of monitoring, measurement, analysis and improvement processes to include the determination of applicable methods.
- Clause 8.2.4 of ISO 9001 prohibits product release and service delivery proceeding until all the planned arrangements have been satisfactorily completed, unless otherwise approved by a **relevant authority**, and where applicable by the customer.

Application

The onus is on the organization to establish what is and what is not applicable. In the context of documents, it is not simply *the document* but *the content*. Only the content addresses the issue in question. The version of the document may be relevant to determining applicability.

Regarding regulations, the organization needs to research the relevant database or library to discover which regulations apply. Clearly, regulations produced for organic material are not applicable to inorganic materials and, therefore, when searching the data, the stated purpose and applicability is important in determining what applies in your situation. For the same reason it is important that your own documents clearly state their applicability. Reliance on titles alone can be misleading.

When scanning regulations and laws, it is important to detect the *applicability clause*. It may not be under a heading but buried in the preamble or introduction. Applicability statements impose boundary conditions: they define the context.

Appropriate

Meaning

Appropriate means suitable for a particular situation, person, product, location, organization, etc.

ISO 9000 requirements and recommendations

There are many uses of the word appropriate in the standard. Here are just a few to illustrate usage:

- Clause 5.3 of ISO 9001 – top management is required to ensure that the quality policy is appropriate to the **purpose of the organization**.
- Clause 5.5.3 of ISO 9001 – top management is required to ensure that appropriate communication processes are established within the organization.
- Clause 6.2.1 of ISO 9001 – personnel performing work affecting product quality are required to be competent on the basis of appropriate education, training, skills and experience.
- Clause 7.3.1 of ISO 9001 requires the organization to determine the review, verification and validation that are appropriate to each design and development stage during design and development planning.
- Clause 7.3.3 of ISO 9001 – design and development outputs are required to provide appropriate information for purchasing, production and for service provision.

Application

The onus is on the organization to determine what is and what is not appropriate. However, unlike the word 'applicable' when the question of applicability is a technical one, determining appropriateness can be subjective. An obvious case is where something might be inappropriate, such as insisting that every action and decision is documented when it has not been proven that this is essential for the organization to meet its objectives. If the organization were a police force, for instance, such a requirement might be prudent because of the legal implications.

If what has been provided does not fulfil the intended purpose, it is unsuitable for the situation and, therefore, not appropriate. The key to determining appropriateness is, therefore, to define the purpose, then select the activity, policy, requirement, etc. that fulfils that purpose.

Approved

Meaning

Approved means that something has been confirmed as meeting prescribed requirements.

ISO 9000 requirements and recommendations

- Clause 7.3.3 of ISO 9001 requires design and development input to be approved prior to release.
- Clause 7.3.7 of ISO 9001 requires design and development changes to be approved before implementation.
- Clause 8.2.4 of ISO 9001 – uncompleted product and service delivery may not proceed unless approved by a **relevant authority**.
- Clause 7.4.1 of ISO 9001 – purchasing information is required to describe requirements for approval of product, procedures, processes and equipment.
- Clause 7.5.2 of ISO 9001 – the organization is required to define criteria for review and approval of special processes and equipment.
- Clause 4.2.3 of ISO 9001 – a documented procedure is required to be established to define the controls needed to approve documents for adequacy prior to issue and re-approve documents following updating.

Application

Anyone can approve something but, for the approval to have any validity, the person granting approval should be recognized as capable of exercising sound judgement within the field of knowledge concerned. Approval by someone who knows nothing about what he/she is approving is worthless. 'Approved' is not the same as '**authorized**': a person may approve a document but not be authorized to do so. Likewise, a person may authorize the use of a document but may not have approved it (because the document may have been approved by someone else).

Assessment

Meaning

In the context of quality management, assessment means the act of determining the extent of compliance with requirements together with the specification of actions necessary to fulfil requirements for compliance.

ISO 9000 requirements and recommendations

- Clause 0.1 of ISO 9001 – the Standard can be used by internal and external parties, including certification bodies, to assess the organization's ability to meet customer, regulatory and the organization's own requirements.
- Clause 5.6.1 of ISO 9001 – the management review is required to include assessing opportunities for improvement.
- Clause 7.6 of ISO 9001 – the organization is required to assess and record the validity of the previous measuring results when the equipment is found not to conform to requirements.

There is no requirement for an organization to carry out an assessment of their suppliers. However, they are required to **evaluate** their suppliers, which is a little different.

- Clause 2.8.2 of ISO 9000 – it is recommended that audit findings be used to assess the **effectiveness of the quality management system** and to identify opportunities for improvement. (This implies that audits produce data for use in assessments.)

Application

Assessment goes further than verification as it involves the determination of actions necessary to make the assessed entity compliant. Therefore, in assessing opportunities for improvement, you would not only identify such opportunities but also make some judgement on the benefits to be gained and the actions to be taken to realize the improvements. In assessing previous measurement results you would determine the impact of invalid measurements and identify the actions to be taken.

Assessor

Meaning

An assessor is a person who makes a judgement on the basis of the findings of an audit. **Auditors** make recommendations not judgements. An analogy is the difference between a tax inspector and a tax assessor. A tax assessor will determine the amount of tax you should pay and a tax auditor will verify the accuracy of the accounts submitted.

ISO 9000 requirements and recommendations

There are no requirements or recommendations in ISO 9000 for assessors.

Application

When the ISO 9000 certification schemes were launched, the personnel performing the audits were known as assessors and continue to be called assessors in many cases. If the auditor determines conformity and then makes a judgement of the system's effectiveness, the auditor is in fact performing an assessment. However, auditors often leave judgement of effectiveness to others.

What you call the personnel performing assessments is up to you. You may call them auditors, inspectors, or analysts, or it may be a role performed by anyone in the organization rather than a specific job. (See also **roles.**)

Assurance

Meaning

Assurance is evidence (verbal or written) that gives confidence that something will/will not happen or has/has not happened. (See also **quality assurance.**)

ISO 9000 requirements and recommendations

ISO 9001 specifies requirements for a quality management system where an organization aims to enhance customer satisfaction through the assurance of conformity to customer and applicable regulatory requirements.

Application

Assurance gives confidence; therefore, you can set up processes that assess operations and gather evidence that the operations are functioning as intended. Assurance activities cannot operate without the operations they serve being planned or executed. Operations may function without assurance activities being present. The assurance activities are, therefore, not essential for the operations to function as intended. However, some operational activities generate evidence that can be used for control and assurance purposes. If the evidence is inadequate for assurance purposes, additional measures need to be taken to install the appropriate provisions that will generate the necessary evidence. For example, in a small organization, there is trust between its members and, therefore, they do not have to prove to others that what they are doing is acceptable. If an external body requires assurance of what they are doing, some additional measures will need to be taken to provide the necessary confidence to this body. This is why ISO 9000 became a burden on the small businesses. These additional activities only existed to satisfy a third party.

Audit

Meaning

An audit is an examination of results to verify their accuracy by someone other than the person responsible for producing them. Audits are a means of verification and, as such, involve monitoring and measurement.

The ISO definition is a 'systematic, independent and documented process for obtaining audit evidence and evaluating it objectively to determine the extent to which **audit criteria** are fulfilled'.

ISO 9000 requirements and recommendations

Clause 8.2.2 of ISO 9001 – the organization is required to:

- Conduct internal audits at planned intervals.
- Define in a documented procedure the responsibilities and requirements for planning and conducting audits.

Application

There are several types of audit, all of which serve a similar purpose but differ in their context: **process audit**, **product audit**, **project audit**, **strategic audit**, **implementation audit**, **internal audit**, **policy audit**, **second-party audit**, **system audit** and **third-party audit**.

Audits follow a common sequence:

- Preparation of audit programme.
- Selection of auditors and a team leader, if necessary.
- Planning the audit.
- Conducting the audit consisting of:
  - (a) opening the meeting, where the criteria, scope and programme of the audit are confirmed;
  - (b) interviews (inspections or tests in the case of product audits) to gather evidence of compliance with prescribed requirements;
  - (c) recording observations;
  - (d) analysis of audit results;
  - (e) preparation of a preliminary audit report;
  - (f) closing the meeting, where results are reported and agreement to actions are confirmed.

- Determining corrective actions.
- Implementing corrective actions.
- Confirming the effectiveness of corrective actions.
- Finalizing the audit report.

Audit criteria

Meaning

The ISO definition is a 'set of policies, procedures or other requirements against which collected audit evidence is compared'.

ISO 9000 requirements and recommendations

Clause 8.2.1 of ISO 9001 requires that the audit criteria, scope, frequency and methods are defined.

Application

Audit criteria are not the same as audit objectives. The audit criteria are the requirements used to measure achievement of the objectives. When planning an audit, you need to identify the documents that contain the criteria against which performance will be judged. In an external audit, this may be ISO 9001, QS-9000, AS 9001, ISO/TS 16949 or other quality management system standard. It could be a product specification if you are conducting a product audit or a process specification if you are auditing a process.

Audit programme

Meaning

The ISO definition of an audit programme is a 'set of one or more audits planned for a specific time frame and directed toward a specific purpose'. You may, therefore, maintain several different audit programmes as the purpose of each audit may vary.

ISO 9000 requirements and recommendations

Clause 8.2.2 of ISO 9001 requires an audit programme to be planned, taking into consideration the **status and importance** of the processes and areas to be audited.

Application

Audit programmes may be needed for auditing systems, processes, products, services, contracts or projects. Each will be on a different timeframe.

The audit programme should include:

- The activity, function, department, process, etc. to be audited.
- The objective of the audit.
- Who has been selected to conduct/lead the audit.
- When the audit is to be conducted.
- The resources required to conduct the audit, when appropriate.

Audit results

Meaning

The results of the audit are all the findings of the audit.

ISO 9000 requirements and recommendations

- Clause 5.6.2 of ISO 9001 – the input to management review is required to include information on results of audits.
- Clause 8.5.1 of ISO 9001 – the organization is required to improve the **effectiveness of the quality management system** continually through the use of audit results.
- Clause 8.2.2 of ISO 9001 – an audit programme is required to be planned, taking into consideration the results of previous audits.

Application

When reporting the results, report and record:

- Those activities or characteristics that were checked.
- Those activities or characteristics that were not checked.
- Those activities or characteristics that were compliant.
- Those activities or characteristics that did not comply.
- Those activities or characteristics where there were opportunities for improvement.

Audit scope

Meaning

The ISO definition of audit scope is 'a description of the extent and boundaries of an audit, in terms of physical locations, organization units, activities and processes as well as the time period covered'.

ISO 9000 requirements and recommendations

Clause 8.2.2 of ISO 9001 – the audit scope is required to be defined.

Application

The scope of the audit is one issue upon which there is most debate. It all comes down to expectations. If you are clear and precise in your definition of scope to begin with, there will be no problems later on. If the organization declares the scope of the management system and seeks certification to ISO 9001, the auditor will judge what should be within the scope of the audit. It could be that the organization has excluded certain parts of the organization when such parts cannot be excluded. For example, product design may be excluded from the scope but the organization designs its own products and, therefore, it should be within the scope.

A simple test of scope is to ask of the organization 'Is there any process or function within this organization that does not contribute directly or indirectly to satisfying customers?'. The answer you receive depends on the person's perception of the role of various functions in the organization. In a service organization:

- Customer satisfaction depends upon service availability.
- Service availability depends upon staff availability.

- Staff availability depends upon staff motivation.
- Staff **motivation** depends upon employee satisfaction.
- Employee satisfaction depends upon pay and conditions.

Therefore, if the management were to sour their relationship with the employees when negotiating pay and conditions, and the staff were to walk out on strike, customer satisfaction would be affected immediately (see **system**).

All functions ultimately contribute to customer satisfaction. The reception area, switchboard, transport, accounts, public relations and other support functions, although not producing deliverable product or service, often interface with customers and have the potential to dissatisfy them, or impact those that do interface with customers or produce product for customers.

Auditors

Meaning

The ISO definition of an auditor is 'a person qualified and appointed to conduct audits'.

ISO 9000 requirements and recommendations

Clause 8.2.2 of ISO 9001 states that auditors cannot audit their own work.

Application

Anyone can perform an audit. If a person audits his or her own work, it is classed as a self-audit. However, self-audits cannot be offered in response to the requirements of ISO 9001: audits have to be independent. If someone has personally produced a piece of work, they are more likely to be biased and oblivious to any deficiencies than someone totally unconnected with the work.

Auditors, like any other personnel, should be competent and, therefore, should possess the required skills and knowledge. However, a person who has only undertaken auditor training is more likely to be a novice. Only after repeated practice under supervision can an auditor be considered trained. An auditor may be classed as competent when he/she has demonstrated a capability to achieve certain defined results with consistency.

Authority

Meaning

Authority is the right to take actions and make decisions.

ISO 9000 requirements and recommendations

- Clause 5.5.1 of ISO 9001 requires top management to ensure that the authorities (of personnel and functions) are defined and communicated within the organization.
- Clause 5.6 of ISO 9001 requires the management representative to have authority that includes:
  (a) ensuring that processes needed for the quality management system are established, implemented and maintained;

(b) reporting to top management on the performance of the quality management system and any need for improvement, and

(c) ensuring the promotion of **awareness** of customer requirements throughout the organization.

Application

The term 'responsibility' is commonly used informally to imply an obligation that a person has to others. However, the term 'authority' has increasingly become associated with power and public bodies, but in principle one cannot have responsibility without authority and vice versa. Problems arise when these two are not matched, where one is greater or less than the other.

In the management context, it constitutes a form of influence and a right to take action, to direct and co-ordinate the actions of others and to use discretion in the position occupied by an individual, rather than in the individuals themselves. Authority is passed downwards in the organization by a process of delegation. All authority rests with the person at the head of the organization until it is delegated. As authority is a right to do something, once delegated, the manager loses the right to take those actions and decisions that have been delegated. The *delegation of authority* permits decisions to be made more rapidly by those who are in more direct contact with the problem. There is simply *no point in employing a dog and barking yourself.* If the dog doesn't bark when it is supposed to, either train the dog to bark or replace the dog with one that does!

Authority should be defined in terms of the actions and decisions a person is permitted to take. Such definitions can be included in policies, job descriptions, procedures or terms of reference.

Authorized

Meaning

Authorized means a permit to do something, enter somewhere or use something.

ISO 9000 requirements and recommendations

There is no requirement in ISO 9001 for anything to be authorized as such, but there are several requirements for approval by a **relevant authority**.

Application

It is prudent when signing documents to indicate whether the signature denotes **approval** or authorization, as they are not one and the same. Anything can be authorized. Authorized does not imply something or someone has been approved. For example, items may be *authorized for use* that are incomplete, nonconforming or otherwise substandard. Prevailing circumstances may dictate such a course of action. Personnel may be authorized to do things that are outside their terms of reference but, equally, when someone is given approved terms of reference, they will be authorized to carry out the duties that are prescribed therein.

Authorization is usually given in writing so as to protect the person taking the action. Authorization is denoted by a signature or stamp of the relevant authority on a document.

Awareness

Meaning

In the context of ISO 9000, awareness is a condition in which a person is informed and knowledgeable about the relevance, importance and consequences of what they do, and the contribution they make to the organization's objectives.

ISO 9000 requirements and recommendations

- Clause 5.5.2 of ISO 9001 requires the management representative to ensure the promotion of awareness of customer requirements throughout the organization.
- Clause 6.2.2 of ISO 9001 requires the organization to ensure that its personnel are aware of the relevance and importance of their activities, and how they contribute to the achievement of the quality objectives.
- Clause 5.1.2 of ISO 9004 states that top management should **demonstrate leadership** in and commitment to promoting policies and objectives to increase awareness, **motivation** and **involvement of people** in the organization.
- Clause 6.2.2 of ISO 9004 recommends that education and training should include awareness of the consequences to the organization and its people of failing to meet the requirements.
- Clause 7.4.2 of ISO 9004 recommends that the organization ensures supplier awareness of and compliance with relevant statutory and regulatory requirements.

Application

All activities impact the organization in some way and the quality of results depends on how they are perceived by the person performing them. In the absence of clear direction, personnel use intuition, instinct, knowledge and experience to the select activities they perform and how they should behave. Awareness of the relevance of an activity means that individuals are more able to select the right activities to perform in a given context. Awareness of the importance of an activity means that individuals are able to approach the activity with the appropriate behaviour. Awareness of the contribution personnel make to the organization means that individuals are able to apportion their efforts accordingly. Awareness of the consequences of what people do means they become more sensitive to failure and its impact upon the organization's customers.

Ways of building awareness include:

- Advising staff before an event of the type of actions and behaviours that are considered appropriate.
- Advising staff during or immediately after an event that their action or behaviour is inappropriate.
- Explaining the purpose of controls and their relationship with performance.
- Explaining preventive action techniques and how to use them.
- Providing induction to a new job.
- Providing training for a new or changed job.
- Providing product briefings.
- Chart displays and warning notices.
- Informing staff of the organization's performance results.

- Providing videos showing activities in context, where components are used, safety incidents, etc.
- Coaching of personnel by demonstrating appropriate behaviour that they may follow.

It is also a responsibility of designers to convey (through the product specifications) critical features and special customer characteristics. Also production planners or service delivery planners should denote special requirements in planning documents so that staff are alerted to requirements that are critical to customers.

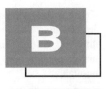

Benchmarking

Meaning

Benchmarking is a technique for measuring an organization's products, services and operations against those of its competitors, resulting in a search for **best practice** that will lead to superior performance.

ISO 9000 requirements and recommendations

There is no requirement for benchmarking in ISO 9001.

- Clause 5.1.1 of ISO 9004 recommends external measurement of the organization's performance, using such methods as benchmarking and third-party evaluation.
- Clause 5.4.1 of ISO 9004 recommends using benchmarking, competitor analysis, and opportunities for improvement when setting quality objectives.
- Clause 5.6.2 of ISO 9004 recommends using results from benchmarking activities as inputs to the management review.
- Clause 7.2 of ISO 9004 recommends the use of benchmarking information when defining processes for **communication with customers** and other interested parties.
- Clause 8.1.2 of ISO 9004 recommends that benchmarking of individual processes should be used as a tool for improving the effectiveness and efficiency of processes.
- Clause 8.4 of ISO 9004 recommends that the results of data analysis should be used for benchmarking the organization's performance.
- Clause 8.5.4 of ISO 9004 recommends that the involvement of people can be achieved by benchmarking competitor performance.

Application

With benchmarking you analyse your current position, find an organization that is performing measurably better and learn from them what they are doing that gives them the competitive edge. You then change your processes as a result of what you learn and then implement the changes.

Caution should be taken not to participate in benchmarking activity that is nothing more than *industrial tourism* and/or copying. The first step in benchmarking, if undertaken, should be to understand the 'what and why' of current performance of your own system or process. That work usually exposes substantial scope for action for improvement.

The organization selected need not to be one in the same line of business because you are benchmarking processes not the whole business. You may find organizations in totally different sectors using similar processes. For example, order processing is common to many organizations. What you need to find is an organization with a similar throughput.

Best practice

Meaning

Best practice is a practice that is both efficient and effective. Best practice is not the best that you can do but the practice that results in people doing the right things right first time.

ISO 9000 requirements and recommendations

There is no requirement for best practice in ISO 9001.

Clause 8.5.4 of ISO 9004 recommends that involvement of people can be achieved through employing best practice.

Application

Best practice results from an evaluation of different ways of doing something and a search for a better way. The search may be internal or may extend outside the business. The organization using the best practice of all those evaluated becomes the **benchmark** against which all others are measured.

Breakthrough

Meaning

A breakthrough is a decisive movement towards new higher levels of performance. Breakthrough is one of two ways to conduct continual process improvement.

ISO 9000 requirements and recommendations

- Clause 5.1.2 of ISO 9004 recommends that, in addition to small-step or ongoing continual improvement, top management should also consider breakthrough changes to processes as a way to improve the organization's performance.
- Clause 8.2.2 of ISO 9004 recommends that measurements should be used for evaluation of the processes that may be suitable for breakthrough projects.
- Clause 8.5.1 of ISO 9004 suggests that improvements can range from small-step ongoing continual improvement to strategic breakthrough improvement projects.
- Clause 8.5.4 of ISO 9000 recommends that management should support improvements in the form of small-step ongoing activities integral to existing processes as well as breakthrough opportunities, in order to gain maximum benefit for the organization and interested parties.

- Annex B of ISO 9004 recommends that breakthrough projects should be conducted in an effective and efficient way using project management methods.

Application

A breakthrough in performance is achieved through a universal series of steps:

1 Determine the objective to be achieved, e.g. new markets, products or technologies, or new levels of organizational efficiency or managerial effectiveness, new national standards or government legislation. These provide the reasons for needing change.
2 Determine the policies needed for improvement, i.e. the broad guidelines to enable management to cause or stimulate the improvement.
3 Conduct a feasibility study. This should discover whether accomplishment of the objective is feasible and propose several strategies or conceptual solutions for consideration. If feasible, approval to proceed should be secured.
4 Produce plans for the improvement that specifies the means by which the objective will be achieved.
5 Organize the resources to implement the plan.
6 Carry out research, analysis and design to define a possible solution and credible alternatives.
7 Model and develop the best solution and carry out tests to prove it fulfils the objective.
8 Identify and overcome any resistance to the change in standards.
9 Implement the change, i.e. put new products into production and new services into operation.
10 Put in place the controls to hold the new level of performance.

Business management process

Meaning

Business management is one of the core **business processes**. It creates the **mission, vision** and overall strategy for the organization, and develops the processes needed to fulfil the goals. It is within the business management process that the **business management system** is conceived, developed and improved.

ISO 9000 requirements and recommendations

There are no requirements or recommendations in ISO 9000 for a business management process. However, there are requirements governing organization purpose, objectives, policies, process identification and development, management review, customer-satisfaction monitoring and continual improvement – all of which come within the scope of a business management process.

Application

It was stated in 'ISO 9000 in a nutshell' that requirements should not be taken in isolation. There are linkages to be made and, by making these linkages, a business management process is defined. A model business management process is illustrated in the figure.

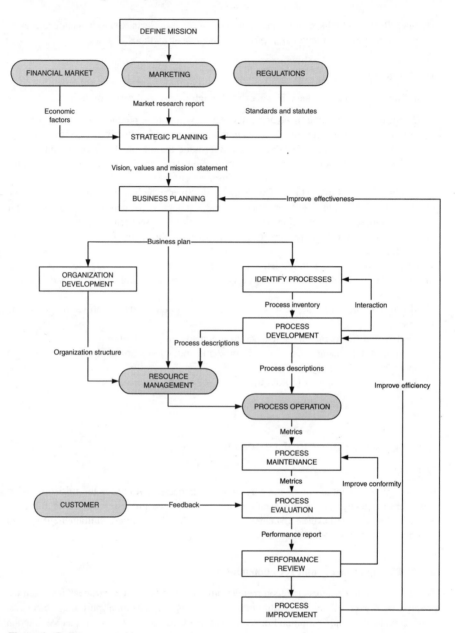

Figure 4   Business management process

Business management system

The business management **system** is the collection of interconnected **business processes** that
enable the organization to achieve its **objectives**. The terms business management system and
quality management system are synonymous.

As quality is defined in ISO 9000 as 'the degree to which a set of inherent characteristics fulfils a need or expectation that is stated, generally implied or obligatory', it follows that all business outputs have characteristics that are intended to fulfil needs and, therefore, the system which delivers these outputs must be a business management system.

ISO 9004 focuses on all **interested parties**. It is a business management system that will deliver outputs that satisfy these interested parties. ISO 9001 focuses on one of these interested parties, the customer, and, therefore, when assessing a BMS against ISO 9001, not all of the system will be examined.

Business process

Meaning

A business process is a process that delivers business outputs (see also **functions**). They are the means by which an organization serves its stakeholders. Everything that the organization does should fit into one or more of these processes so that they cover the organization's entire scope of work both operationally and administratively.

Business processes often comprise subprocesses and work processes that interact to deliver business outputs.

ISO 9000 requirements and recommendations

There are no requirements or recommendations in ISO 9000 for business processes simply because the standard is generic and applicable to all types of organizations, not just businesses.

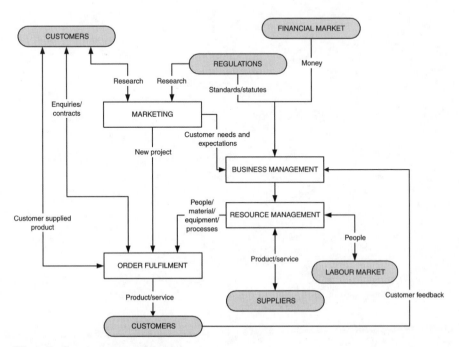

Figure 5   Generic system model

Application

For processes to be classed as business processes they need to be in a chain of processes having the same stakeholder at each end of the chain. The input is an input to the business and the output is an output from the business, so that the outputs can be measured in terms of the inputs. Normally, organizations have few business processes because there are few types of output that require different processes. However, organizations that provide a range of different services may indeed have several business processes. A system model showing the core business processes is illustrated in the figure.

Business processes are defined through **process descriptions**. **Marketing**, **order fulfilment**, **business management** and **resource management** processes are defined elsewhere in this book.

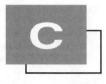

Calibration

Meaning

Calibrate means to standardize the quantities of a measuring instrument. Calibration is a process that establishes under specified conditions, the relationship between values indicated by a measuring instrument and the corresponding values of a quantity realized by a reference standard. When the values of both measuring instrument and reference standard are normalized or recorded, the instrument is said to be calibrated.

ISO 9000 requirements and recommendations

Clause 7.6 of ISO 9001 requires measuring equipment to be calibrated or verified at specified intervals, or prior to use, against measurement standards traceable to international or national measurement standards.

Application

In order to establish whether a device requires calibration you need to ask 'What is it used for?'. It is not necessary to calibrate all measuring and monitoring devices. Some devices may be used solely as an indicator, such as a thermometer, a clock or a tachometer. Other equipment may be used for diagnostic purposes, to indicate whether or not a fault exists. If such devices are not used for determining the acceptability of products and services or **process parameters**, their calibration is not essential. Devices such as steel rules only require inspection for damage – their accuracy does not deteriorate with age.

Some devices, if well treated and retained in a controlled environment, will retain their accuracy for very long periods. Others, if poorly treated and subjected to environmental extremes, will lose their accuracy very quickly. Ideally, you should calibrate measuring devices subject to drift before use (in order to prevent an inaccurate device being used in the first place) and afterwards (to confirm that no changes have occurred during use).

Certification

Meaning

Certification is a process by which a product, process, person or organization is deemed to meet specified requirements.

ISO 9000 requirements and recommendations

- Clause 0.3 of ISO 9001 states that the standard specified requirements can be used for certification purposes.
- Clause 1 of ISO 9004 states that ISO 9004 is not intended for certification use.

There are no requirements for certification in ISO 9001.

Application

Following a verification, audit or **assessment**, if the entity verified, audited or assessed were found to meet the specified requirements, you would declare this on a certificate in the following form:

> We hereby declare that the (item, organization) has been (assessed, audited, verified) and unless otherwise specified hereon has been found to conform to the requirements of (acceptance criteria – issue and date).

Certification body

Meaning

A certification body is an organization that conducts certification of conformity. Organizations that have **demonstrated** conformity with prescribed standards are deemed to be certificated. They are not **accredited**; this is the status of certification bodies that demonstrate conformity with prescribed standards.

ISO 9000 requirements and recommendations

Clause 0.1 of ISO 9001 states that the standard can be used by certification bodies to assess the organization's ability to meet customer, regulatory and the organization's own requirements.

There are no requirements or recommendations in ISO 9000 addressing certification bodies.

Application

Should you choose to obtain certification for your organization, you will need to select an appropriate certification body. There are dozens of bodies to choose from, but not all may be accredited in the sector in which your organization operates. Certification bodies are accredited by standard industry classification codes (SIC codes) or NACE code. The SIC is a coding system which classifies businesses by their main type of economic activity. The codes can be found at: http://www.osti.gov/waisgate/padsfldhelp.sic.html. The European equivalent is NACE. NACE codes can be found at: http://www.econ.ucl.ac.be/IRES/BASE_DE_DONNEES/Nomenclatures/CITI_ISIC/ISIC Rev3.html.

Not all certification bodies are accredited and, of those that are accredited, not all are accredited by a national **accreditation body**. There are general certification bodies such as Lloyds Register Quality Assurance (LRQA) that possess accreditation to a wide range of SIC codes and industry-specific certification bodies, such as the Ceramic Industry Certification Scheme (CICS), which serves the ceramics industry.

The majority are commercial in that they are funded from certification fees. In some respects this means they are less independent than an organization that is funded by government. There can, therefore, be a conflict when failing a client might mean losing a customer and, therefore, revenue. To overcome this problem, certification bodies provide improvement services to their clients in the form of training courses, seminars, publications and help desks, which must be impartial, otherwise they will lose their right to practise. The conditions of accreditation are that a certification body is not permitted to provide consulting services. However, many overcome this obstacle by setting up a separate consulting business with no financial links between the two operations. This is a little like the school inspector being employed by the school governors. If you want genuine independent advice, it might be prudent to choose a provider that is not in the certification business.

Codes of practice

Meaning

Codes of practice are a systematically arranged and comprehensive collection of rules, regulations or principles.

ISO 9000 requirements and recommendations

Clause 7.3.2 of ISO 9004 recommends that industry codes of practice be used in defining design inputs.

Application

Codes of practice tend to be expressed as instructions on what to do and what not to do in certain situations. They are not procedures in that they do not, in general, tell you how to do something unless there is a standard method for a task. The order in which the instructions are presented is by topic rather than a sequence in which the instructions would be implemented in practice. They are, therefore, suitable for imparting knowledge, alerting people to dangers and ensuring the factors critical to success are addressed. To be effective, codes of practice need to be learnt or built into designs, processes and procedures. They cannot function effectively without some intermediate mechanism that translates the rules into action.

Collection of data

Meaning

Data are generated during the operation of every process. Some data may be recorded and transmitted to subsequent process stages for process control purposes. Other data may not be essential for process control but are needed for process improvement. In both cases, provision needs to be made for these data to be collected.

ISO 9000 requirements and recommendations

Clause 8.4 of ISO 9001 requires the organization to:

- collect appropriate data to **demonstrate** the suitability and **effectiveness of the QMS**; and
- collect appropriate data to evaluate where continual improvement of the effectiveness of the QMS can be made.

Application

In order to **analyse data**, you must first of all make arrangements for the right kind of data to be collected. Therefore, only collect data on events that you intend to analyse. Your analysis will only be as good as the data with which you are provided. You also need to take care to avoid the *garbage in/garbage out* syndrome.

Data collection may involve any or all of the following actions:

- Identifying the key parameters to be measured.
- Determining the processes from which information is to be gathered.
- Locating where in the process the data are generated.
- Determining the method of data collection – the instruments, forms, questionnaires, interview check lists to be used, etc.
- Determining the frequency of data collection.
- Identifying the personnel or the instrumentation that will collect the data.
- Establishing communication channels to route the data to those responsible for the data analysis, or setting up the equipment to receive the data and perform the analysis.
- Describing the data collection methods in the process descriptions.
- Gathering the data.
- Routing the data to those responsible for its analysis.

Commitment

Meaning

A commitment is an obligation that a person (or a company) takes on in order to do something. A commitment exists if a person agrees to do something and informs others of their intentions. A commitment that is not communicated is merely a personal commitment with no obligation, except to one's own conscience.

ISO 9000 requirements and recommendations

- Clause 5.1 of ISO 9001 requires top management to provide evidence of their commitment to the development and implementation of the quality management system and continually improving its **effectiveness**.
- Clause 5.3 of ISO 9001 requires top management to ensure that the quality policy includes a commitment to comply with requirements and continually improve the effectiveness of the quality management system.
- Clause 7.2.2 of ISO 9001 requires the organization to conduct a review of the requirements related to the product prior to a commitment to supply a product to the customer.

Application

In practice commitment means:

- Doing what you need to do to meet the organization's objectives.
- Doing what you say you will do.
- Not accepting work that is below standard.
- Not shipping product that is below standard.
- Not walking by problems, and not overlooking mistakes.
- Honouring plans, procedures, policies and promises.
- Listening to the interested parties.

Stage	Level	Meaning
0	Zero	I do not know anything about it.
1	Awareness	I know what it is and why I should do it.
2	Understanding	I know what I have to do and what I need to do it.
3	Investment	I have the resources to do it and I know how to deploy them.
4	Intent	This is what I am going to do and how I am going to do it.
5	Action	I have completed the first few actions and it has been successful.
6	Commitment	I am now doing everything I said I would do.

Before giving a commitment to anything, people need to be aware of:

- The resources (time, effort, equipment, etc.) required to fulfil that commitment.
- The behaviours that may need to change to cause the right things to happen.
- The priorities that may need to change to meet the commitment.
- The dedication and vigilance required to initiate action, maintain progress and prevent failure.
- The impact on others.
- The consequences of pulling out, deviating from or compromising intentions.

Commitments are expressed by the words 'we will', 'we are', 'we do', 'we don't', and 'we have'.

There are seven stages towards commitment (see table).

Common cause variation

Meaning

The random variation present in a process that is due to factors that are inherent in the system.

ISO 9000 requirements and recommendations

There are no requirements in ISO 9000 addressing common cause variation but there are requirements for corrective action. Corrective action is concerned with removal of variation due to **special causes** and common causes that cause variation beyond the specification limits.

Application

Variation is present in all systems. Nothing is absolutely stable. Conditions may appear stable but, if the sensitivity of the measuring device is increased, variation will be detected. If you monitor the difference between the measured value and the required value of a characteristic and plot it on a horizontal timescale in the order the products were produced, you would notice that there is variation over time. There does not have to be a required value to spot variation.

Common cause variation is random and, therefore, adjusting a process on detection of a common cause will destabilize the process.

The random variation is caused by factors that are inherent in the system. The operator has done all he or she can to remove the **special causes**, the rest are left to the management. This variation could be caused by poor design, working environment, equipment maintenance or inadequacy of information. Some of these events may be common to all processes, all machines, all materials of a particular type, all work performed in a particular location or environment, or all work performed using a particular method.

Competence

Meaning

If a person has the appropriate education, training and skills to perform a job, the person can be considered qualified. If a person demonstrates the ability to achieve the desired results, the person can be considered competent. Competence is, therefore, the ability to **demonstrate** *use* of education, skills and behaviours to achieve the results required for a job.

ISO 9000 requirements and recommendations

- Clause 4.2.1 of ISO 9001 states that the extent of the quality management system documentation can differ from one organization to another, owing to the competence of personnel.
- Clause 6.2.2 of ISO 9001 requires the organization to determine the necessary competence for personnel performing work affecting product quality.
- Clause 6.1.2 of ISO 9004 recommends that consideration should be given to resources to improve the performance of the organization, such as enhancement of competence via focused training, education and learning.
- Clause 6.2.2.1 ISO 9004 recommends that management should:
  - (a) ensure that the necessary competence is available for the effective and efficient operation of the organization;
  - (b) consider analysis of both the present and expected competence needs as compared to the competence already existing in the organization; and
  - (c) evaluate the competence of individual people to perform defined activities.
- Clause 6.2.2.2 of ISO 9004 recommends that the objective of planning for education and training needs is to provide people with knowledge and skills, which, together with experience, improve their competence.
- Clause 7.1.3.2 of ISO 9004 recommends that the competence of people is a factor in developing an effective and efficient plan for controlling and monitoring the activities within the organization's processes.
- Clause 8.3.2 of ISO 9004 recommends that people carrying out the review of nonconformities should have the competence to evaluate the total effects of the nonconformity.

Application

In any organization, there are positions that people occupy, jobs they carry out and roles they perform in these positions. For each of these, certain outcomes are required from the occupants. There are, therefore, a number of steps to take in ensuring personnel are competent.

1 Define the outcomes required from a job (the tangible issues, such as product quality and throughput, as well as the soft issues, such as behaviours, influence and stamina). This answers the question 'What must be achieved?'.
2 Define what makes those performing it successful and agree these with the role/job holder. This answers the question 'What must be done for this to be achieved?'.
3 Define the performance criteria, This answers the question 'How well must this be done?'.
4 Define the method of assessment. This answers the questions 'How will we measure competence?', 'When will we measure it?' and 'Where will we measure it?'.
5 Define the evidence required to demonstrate competence. This answers the question 'What should we measure and what will we record?'.
6 Define the responsibilities. This answers the question 'Who will perform the assessment?'.
7 Perform competence assessment.
8 Collect the evidence.
9 Match evidence to performance criteria.
10 Record and report the findings.
11 Provide the education and training consistent with enabling the individual concerned to achieve the agreed standards.

Concession

Meaning

In the context of quality management, a concession is permission granted by an acceptance authority to supply product or service that does not meet the prescribed requirements.

ISO 9000 requirements and recommendations

- Clause 8.3 of ISO 9001 requires the organization to deal with nonconforming product by authorizing acceptance under concession by a **relevant authority** when appropriate.
- Clause 8.3 of ISO 9001 requires records of concessions obtained to be maintained.

Application

You would only apply for a concession to deliver nonconforming product if you really believed that the nonconformity did not affect fit, form or function. If these parameters are affected, you run the risk of interchangeability or interface problems through the supply chain. Concessions are generally limited to specified time periods and quantities. They are not authority to deviate from the specification for anything other than the items and quantities specified.

The concession is normally submitted to the acceptance authority for the items concerned. If the variation is from internal specification, the acceptance authority will be internal personnel. If the variation also departs from customer or regulatory requirement, the acceptance authority will be an external body, such as the customer's design or QA authority or the government-appointed regulator for the industry sector concerned. External concessions should not occur, but there may be circumstances with certain contracts and projects where some flexibility is needed.

When delivering the product that is the subject of a concession, it is prudent to quote the concession on the accompanying documentation otherwise the item may be rejected on receipt.

Continual improvement

Meaning

In ISO 9000:2000, continual improvement is defined as 'a recurring activity to increase the ability to fulfil requirements'. This implies that any beneficial change is improvement: that resolving problems which should not have arisen is *improvement*! Juran and Deming say that putting out fires is not improvement of the process, neither is discovery and removal of a **special cause** detected by a point out of control. This only puts the process back to where it should have been in the first place. If there is no status quo (no normal level), action needs to be taken to establish a normal level, i.e. bring operations under control. You can only improve what is already under control. Bringing operations under control is not improvement.

Process control and continual improvement are two distinct concepts. Continual improvement is about improving the efficiency and effectiveness of products, processes and systems that are already under control. Process control is about maintaining variation in a process at a level where the only variation present is random and the process is stable and, therefore, predictable.

Continual improvement is one of the eight quality management principles and is explained as follows: 'Continual improvement of the organization's overall performance should be a permanent objective of the organization'.

ISO 9000 requirements and recommendations

Continual improvement appears in many places in both ISO 9001 and ISO 9004; therefore, only a selection of references is given here.

- Clause 4.1 of ISO 9001 requires the organization to continually improve the effectiveness of its quality management system.
- Clause 5.3 of ISO 9001 requires top management to ensure that the quality policy includes a **commitment** to continually improve the **effectiveness of the quality management** system.
- Clause 6.1 of ISO 9001 requires the organization to determine and provide the resources needed to continually improve the effectiveness of the quality management system.
- Clause 8.1 of ISO 9001 requires the organization to plan and implement the monitoring, measurement, analysis and improvement processes needed to continually improve the effectiveness of the quality management system.
- Clause 8.4 of ISO 9001 requires the organization to evaluate where continual improvement of the quality management system can be made.
- Clause 5.1.2 of ISO 9004 recommends that top management establish continual improvement as an objective for processes of the organization and consider breakthrough changes to processes as a way to improve the organization's performance.
- Clause 6.6 of ISO 9004 recommends encouraging suppliers to implement programmes for continual improvement of performance and to participate in other joint improvement initiatives.
- Clause 8.5.1 of ISO 9004 recommends that improvements can range from small-step ongoing continual improvement to strategic breakthrough improvement projects.

Application

An organization applying the continual improvement principles would be one in which people are:

- Making continual improvement of products, processes and systems an objective for every individual in the organization.
- Applying the basic improvement concepts of incremental improvement and breakthrough improvement.
- Using periodic assessments against established criteria of excellence to identify areas for potential improvement.
- Continually improving the efficiency and effectiveness of all processes.
- Promoting prevention-based activities.
- Providing every member of the organization with appropriate education and training, on the methods and tools of continual improvement.
- Establishing measures and goals to guide and track improvements.
- Recognizing improvements.

To undertake continual improvement, the process must be under control to start with. The **special cause variation** must have been removed. Elimination of special causes requires the **corrective action** process.

The process output must meet the objectives. So if you planned to achieve 75 per cent on-time delivery, you must be achieving an average of 75 per cent on-time delivery before continual improvement is initiated. If the process only achieved 50 per cent on-time delivery, the objectives are not aligned with the process for achieving them and, therefore, you need to go back and redesign the process. It is futile to set a target that a process cannot meet on the premise that everyone will work harder to achieve the new target. If the process average is 50 per cent after you have removed the special causes, 50 per cent it is. A good place to start, therefore, is to measure the performance of each process and set the targets at the process average.

If you have a 5 per cent defect rate (5 in 100 products are found defective on receipt by the customer), the place to start is to examine the special causes. When these have been eliminated and the process averages a 2 per cent defect rate, you will not improve its performance unless you focus on the **common causes** – the errors due to inherent weaknesses in the system.

Once you have a stable process that is meeting the target, you can focus your achievements on reducing the resources to achieve the target. When resource utilization is at an optimum for the process, improvements can be made by raising the target, e.g. going from 2 per cent defective to 0.2 per cent defective or achieving three sigma. When you have achieved three sigma, you can pursue more improvement to reach **six sigma**. Going from three sigma to six sigma often requires a **breakthrough process**.

Continuous improvement

Meaning

In the context of ISO 9000 there is no difference between continuous improvement and continual improvement. Improvement that is continuous has no periods of stability, it is applied all the time. Although the rate of change may vary, improvement does not stop. In reality, there are periods of stability between periods of change and, therefore, 'continual improvement' is a better term to describe the phenomenon.

The word 'continuous' can be used legitimately in connection with processes or materials. Processes that supply energy from fossil fuel are continuous. We are certainly aware when they stop! Most chemical and food processes are 'continuous' and only stop when demand ceases. Materials that are cut to length on demand, such as paper, wire and carpets, can be classed as 'continuous'.

ISO 9000 requirements and recommendations

The term is not used in ISO 9000.

Application

In the field of quality management the term 'continual improvement' should be used in preference to 'continuous improvement'.

Contract

Meaning

A contract is an agreement formally executed by both customer and supplier (enforceable by law), which requires performance of services or delivery of products at a cost to the customer in accordance with stated terms and conditions.

ISO 9000 requirements and recommendations

- Clause 7.2.2 of ISO 9001 requires the organization to review requirements related to the product prior to its **commitment** to supply a product to the customer (e.g. submission of tenders, acceptance of contracts or orders, acceptance of changes to contracts or orders).
- Clause 7.2.2 of ISO 9001 requires the organization to ensure that contract or order requirements differing from those previously expressed are resolved.
- Clause 7.2.3 of ISO 9001 requires the organization to determine and implement effective arrangements for communicating with customers in relation to contracts.

Application

The primary benefit of a written contract is that it provides a basis for reference. People forget what they agreed months or years afterwards. Sometimes their version of the facts is somewhat different. With a written contract, it outlives the parties shaking hands because it is usually in the name of the corporate bodies. If a representative of one party moves on, the contract still stands. Written contracts are often more appropriate when the terms are complex and where human memory cannot be relied upon. However, if the two parties did not have the same perception of what was being agreed when both parties signed the written contract, the parties may have to do battle in the law courts.

Verbal contracts made on a handshake work when the parties shaking hands outlive the duration of the contract. If one party moves on and a new party succeeds to the position, none of the understanding that made the agreement work is carried over. A new contract has to be made with the new party.

Whether written or verbal, it is wise to enter a contract carefully:

- Do not promise what you or your organization cannot deliver, for you will be caught out.
- Seek definitions for any terms or phrases that might have more than one meaning, e.g. acceptance, delivery, completion, product and specification.
- Establish the boundaries affecting what you and the customer are responsible for.
- Ensure it is clear what each party does, provides, submits, relinquishes, hands over and agrees, and when they do it.

- Establish the conditions for acceptance.
- Define what payment is to be made on completion and when completion is required.
- Read the small print and any reference documents before you accept the contract.
- Declare any areas where your offer differs from that required and state the reasons in terms advantageous to the customer.
- Check that your sources of data, prices, technical specification, etc., are current and applicable to the specific terms of the contract.
- Issue contract amendments on the same distribution list as the original contract.
- Do not imply acceptance of a change to contract in any **communication** other than a formal contract amendment. There could be hidden costs or other implications about which you are unaware.

Control

Meaning

Control is the act of preventing or regulating change in parameters, situations or conditions. Controls prevent change and, when applied to quality, they regulate quality performance and prevent undesirable changes being present in the quality of the product or service being supplied. When operations are under control, they are predictable and predictability is a factor that is vital for any organization to be successful. If you cannot predict what might happen when a process is initiated, you are relying on chance. The quality of products and services cannot be left to chance.

ISO 9000 requirements and recommendations

Control appears in many places in ISO 9000, ISO 9001 and ISO 9004; therefore, only a selection of references is given here.

- Clause 0.2 of ISO 9000 recommends that, in order to lead and operate an organization successfully, it is necessary to direct and control it in a systematic and transparent manner.
- Clause 2.1 of ISO 9000 recommends the organization to analyse customer requirements, define the processes that contribute to the achievement of a product that is acceptable to the customer, and keep these processes under control.
- Clause 4.1 of ISO 9001 requires the organization to determine criteria and methods needed to ensure that control of the processes needed for the quality management system processes are effective.
- Clause 4.1 of ISO 9001 requires the quality management system documentation to include documents needed by the organization to ensure the effective control of its processes.
- Clause 7.3.1 of ISO 9001 requires the organization to control the design and development of product.
- Clause 7.4.1 of ISO 9001 requires the type and extent of control applied to the supplier and the purchased product to be dependent upon the effect of the purchased product on subsequent **product realization** or the final product.
- Clause 7.5.4 of ISO 9001 requires the organization to exercise care with customer property while it is under the organization's control.
- Clause 8.3 of ISO 9001 requires the organization to ensure that product that does not conform to product requirements is identified and controlled to prevent its unintended use or delivery.

Application

For an action to control a situation, the action has to act upon the factors that cause the results. It is for this reason that inspection, test or other methods of verification do not in fact control output – they simply measure it. It is the subsequent action that controls the results. Whether it is to stop delivery, return an item for reprocessing or correct the error, it is these actions that control the output.

To control anything, you need to execute a universal sequence of actions:

1 Determine what parameter is to be controlled.
2 Establish its criticality and whether you need to control it before, during or after results are produced.
3 Establish a specification for the parameter to be controlled, which provides limits of acceptability and units of measure.
4 Produce plans for controls that specify the means by which the characteristics will be achieved, and variation detected and removed.
5 Organize resources to implement the plans for control.
6 Install a sensor at an appropriate point in the process to sense variance from specification.
7 Collect and transmit data to a place for analysis.
8 Verify the results and establish whether the variance is within the range expected for a stable process (the status quo).
9 Diagnose the cause of any variance beyond the expected range.
10 Propose remedies and decide on the action needed to restore the status quo.
11 Take the agreed action and check that process stability has been restored.

Control before, during and after an event

Meaning

- Control before an event is action taken to detect and prevent the occurrence of failure.
- Control during the event is action taken to detect and correct failure as it occurs.
- Control after the event is action taken to detect and correct failure after it has occurred.

ISO 9000 requirements and recommendations

These concepts are not explicit in ISO 9000 but are embodied in such requirements as:

- Planning product realization – control before the event.
- Requirement review – control before the event.
- Control of measuring devices – control before and after the event.
- Document control – control during the event.
- Design review – control during and after the event.
- Measurement of product – control during the event.
- Measurement of process – control during the event.
- Verification of purchased product – control during the event.
- Management review – control before and after the event.
- Management of work environment – control before, during and after the event.

Application

Control before the event is accomplished by predicting failure and taking action to eliminate, reduce or minimize the effects. A tool often used for this is **failure mode and effects analysis** (FMEA).

Control during the event is accomplished by installing sensors in the process that warn of variations outside the limits. The process stops while action is taken to restore the status quo. Several tools are used for this, some are automated and others are manual. Automated tools alert process operators by means of alarms or signals on display panels. Automated controls take action to restore the process to stable conditions. Semi-automated controls require the process operator to take action on being alerted. Manual controls include traditional inspection and test, whether performed by the producer or other personnel, such as a separate inspection and test department. Design reviews, test reviews and document reviews are other examples of control during the event. They all act in-line and the process does not continue until released from the hold point.

Control after the event is accomplished by data collection and analysis. The process continues in an unstable state until the data are analysed and the unacceptable variation detected. Processes in which control relies upon periodic review are typical of this type of control. Management processes fall into this category. The actions do not stop current operations but may well be used to stop further operations when limits are exceeded. Such controls are used where the consequences of failure are less severe or where failure cannot be measured without observing trends over longer periods such as market share, customer satisfaction, sales and overall quality performance.

Control charts

Meaning

A control chart is a graphical comparison of process performance data to computed control limits drawn as limit lines on the chart.

ISO 9000 requirements and recommendations

The term is not used in ISO 9000. However, requirements for the **analysis of data** imply the use of control charts.

Application

A chart that presents performance data alone is not a control chart. Control limits need to be identified on the chart, and performance following a breach of these limits needs to be shown to have changed so as to fall within the limits. A chart with limits and erratic performance is not a control chart – it is simply a performance chart.

Controlled conditions

Meaning

Controlled conditions are arrangements that provide control over all factors that influence the result.

ISO 9000 requirements and recommendations

Clause 7.5.1 of ISO 9001 requires the organization to plan and carry out production and service provision under controlled conditions. Controlled conditions are required to include, as applicable:

- The availability of information that describes the characteristics of the product.
- The availability of **work instructions**.
- The use of suitable equipment.
- The availability and use of monitoring and measuring devices.
- The implementation of monitoring and measurement.
- The implementation of release, delivery and post-delivery activities.

Application

Controlled conditions should prevent undesirable change and, therefore, focus on those factors that might cause change or deviation from what you are trying to do. This is why this clause in ISO 9001 only includes those factors that might impede success.

There are usually eight factors that affect the control of any process:

1 The quality of the people – their competence to do the job with the required proficiency when required. If you cannot identify the competency of personnel required and choose those with the required competence should you need to, you are not in control of the process unless you can compensate by changing other parameters (ISO 9001 Clause 6.2.1).
2 The quality of the physical resources – the capability of plant, machinery, equipment and tools. If you cannot identify the physical resources required and choose or change them should you need to, so that capability is improved, you are not in control of the process (ISO 9001 Clause 7.5.1c).
3 The quality of the physical environment – the level of temperature, cleanliness and vibration. If you cannot identify the physical environment required or change it should you need to, you are not in control of the process (ISO 9001 Clause 6.4).
4 The quality of the human environment – the degree of physical stress, physiological stress and **motivation**. If you cannot identify the human factors required in the work environment required and alter their effect should you need to, you are not in control of the process (ISO 9001 Clause 6.4).
5 The quality of the information – the degree of accuracy, currency, completeness, usability, validity. If you cannot identify the information required and improve its dependability should you need to, you are not in control of the process (ISO 9001 Clause 7.5.1a & b).
6 The quality of materials – the adequacy of physical properties, their consistency and purity. If you cannot identify the materials required and change their properties should you need to, you are not in control of the process (ISO 9001 Clause 7.4).
7 The quantity of resources – time, money, information, people, materials, components, equipment, etc. If you cannot identify the quantities required and adjust them to suit the demand should you need to, you are not in control of the process (ISO 9001 Clause 6.1).
8 The quality of measurement – units, values, timing and integrity. If you cannot identify the measurements to be taken, the units of measure, the target values and when to take them and control the integrity of measurement should you need to, you are not in control of the process (ISO 9001 Clauses 7.5.1d & e and 7.6).

Controlled distribution

Meaning

A controlled distribution is a means of regulating the release of information so that it is received by those who need it. (Ensuring information is received only by those who need it is a **document security**.)

ISO 9000 requirements and recommendations

- Clause 4.2.4 of ISO 9001 requires a documented procedure to be established that defines the controls needed to ensure that documents of external origin are identified and their distribution controlled.
- Clause 4.2.4 of ISO 9001 requires a documented procedure to be established that defines the controls needed to ensure that relevant versions of applicable documents are available at points of use (implying that information distribution needs to be controlled).

Application

Some measure of control can be accomplished with hard copy documents by using copy numbers against named copyholders. This enables documents and any changes to reach nominated personnel. If the positions of these copyholders is stated rather than the named individual, it may ensure continuity when people leave. However, this is no guarantee, as often positions also change when people leave.

With electronically stored information, the nominated personnel either access information from their workstation when they need it or information is released on a prescribed distribution. The difficulty here is that names are often used rather than positions. When the person leaves, the distribution lists need to be changed. This makes maintenance tedious unless the e-mail addresses are organized by position rather than the jobholder's name. The solution is to send short-life information to individuals and long-life information into a server directory, where it can be accessed when needed.

Controlled documents

Controlled documents are documents for which the development, approval, issue, change, distribution, maintenance, use, storage, security, obsolescence or disposal is regulated.

Corrective action

Meaning

Corrective action is action planned or taken to stop something from recurring. It could be a one-off event (**special cause variation**), a recurring event or an inherent condition (**common cause variation**). Corrective action can, therefore, be considered to be an instrument of both process control and process improvement.

Corrective action is the pattern of activities that traces the symptoms of a problem to its cause, produces solutions for preventing the recurrence of the problem, implements the change and monitors that the change has been successful.

A problem has to exist for you to take corrective action. When actual problems do not exist but there is a possibility of a problem occurring, the action of preventing the occurrence of the problem is a **preventive action**.

Corrective action forms part of every process rather than being a separate process. Traceability is required in order to find the root cause of a problem and take corrective action to prevent its recurrence.

Product recall is a remedial action and not a corrective action because it does not prevent a recurrence of the initial problem. Resolving a customer complaint is a remedial action and not a corrective action because it does not prevent a recurrence of the initial problem.

The concept of corrective action is often misunderstood. Corrective action is sometimes believed to be about fixing problems and preventive action about preventing recurrence of problems. This is understandable because synonyms for correction are fix, remedy, rectify and alter. However, corrective action in ISO 9000 has always been about preventing recurrence because **nonconforming product** addressed the correction of problems.

ISO 9000 requirements and recommendations

- Clause 5.6.2 of ISO 9001 requires the input to management review to include information on the status of corrective actions.
- Clause 8.2.3 of ISO 9001 requires correction and corrective action to be taken, as appropriate, when planned results are not achieved to ensure conformity of the product.
- Clause 8.5.2 of ISO 9001 requires corrective actions to be appropriate to the effects of the nonconformities encountered.
- Clause 8.5.2 of ISO 9001 requires a documented corrective action procedure to be established.
- Clause 7.1.3.3 of ISO 9004 recommends that any changes in the process affecting product characteristics should be recorded and communicated in order to maintain the conformity of the product and provide information for corrective action.
- Clause 8.3.2 of ISO 9004 recommends that people carrying out nonconformity review should have the authority and resources to disposition the nonconformity and to define appropriate corrective action.
- Clause 8.5.2 of ISO 9004 recommends that top management should ensure that corrective action is used as a tool for improvement.
- Clause 7.1.3.2 of ISO 9004 recommends that process outputs should be evaluated against input requirements and acceptance criteria to identify necessary corrective actions.
- Clause 8.5.2 of ISO 9004 recommends that corrective action planning includes an evaluation of the significance of problems in terms of the potential impact on such aspects as operating costs, nonconformity costs, product performance, dependability, and the safety and satisfaction of customers and other interested parties.
- Clause 8.5.2 of ISO 9004 advises that there are many ways to determine the causes of nonconformity, including analysis by an individual or the assignment of a corrective-action project team.

Application

Steps in the corrective action process are as follows:

1 Collect the nonconformity data and classify.
2 Conduct a Pareto analysis to identify the vital few and trivial many.
3 Organize a diagnostic team.
4 Postulate causes and test theories.
5 Determine the root cause of nonconformity.
6 Determine the effects of nonconformity and the need for action.

7 Record the criteria for determining severity or priority.
8 Determine the action needed to prevent nonconformity recurring.
9 Organize an implementation team.
10 Create or choose the conditions that will ensure effective implementation.
11 Implement the agreed action.
12 Assess and record the actions taken and record the results.
13 Determine whether the actions were those required to be taken.
14 Determine whether the actions were performed in the best possible way.
15 Determine whether the nonconformity has recurred.
16 If nonconformity has recurred repeat steps 1–15.

Corrective maintenance

Meaning

Corrective maintenance is **maintenance** carried out after a failure has occurred and is intended to restore an item to a state in which it can perform its required function. Corrective maintenance is a remedial action not a corrective action. This may appear illogical but, in the context of ISO 9000, this is the way the terms are defined.

ISO 9000 requirements and recommendations

There are no specific requirements in ISO 9001 for corrective maintenance. However, there are requirements for the maintenance of infrastructure.

Application

The primary objective of corrective maintenance is to minimize down time – the time that equipment is unavailable owing to a malfunction or failure.
  Downtime is a function of:

● response time;
● diagnostic time;
● availability of spare parts and consumables; and
● correction time.

Corrective maintenance needs to be resourced. There are several options from which to choose an appropriate strategy for your organization:

● complete in-house maintenance capability;
● first-line maintenance capability in-house, the rest outsourced;
● consumables replenishment in-house, the rest outsourced; and
● all corrective maintenance outsourced.

Response times will vary depending on your maintenance strategy. Diagnostic and correction time will depend upon the level of in-built diagnostics, the competence of your maintenance personnel and the availability of spares. It is, therefore, necessary to determine your maintenance requirements relative to the impact of down time on your capability to meet customer requirements and design a corrective maintenance process that meets these requirements.

Some of the documentation you may need includes:

- a list of the equipment upon which **process capability** depends;
- procedures dealing with the actions required in the event of equipment malfunction;
- procedures defining how specific maintenance tasks are to be conducted; and
- maintenance logs, which record corrective maintenance work carried out.

Critical success factors

Meaning

Critical success factors are those factors upon which the achievement of specified objectives depend.

ISO 9000 requirements and recommendations

The term is not used in the ISO 9000 family of standards, but there are requirements for objective to be established consistent with the quality policy. Critical success factors need to be known to do this.

Application

Having established the purpose and **mission** of the organization, the next step is to determine the critical success factors (CSFs) as these will identify the areas where objectives need to be set. CSFs are often determined by asking the question 'What factors affect our ability to fulfil our mission?'.

- If our success depends upon the safety of our products, then we need safety objectives.
- If our success depends upon securing the integrity of information entrusted to us by our customers, then we need security objectives.
- If our success depends upon the impact our operations have on the environment, we need environmental objectives.
- If our success depends upon maintaining good relations with the unions, we need industrial relations objectives.
- If something is critical to our success, we should set objectives and design processes for their achievement.

CSFs can be determined at any level, not only when planning the strategic intent of an organization. Whatever the goal, there are factors that affect our ability to achieve it. Often such factors relate to:

- the availability and competence of certain people;
- the availability, quantity and integrity of certain resources;
- the availability and integrity of certain information or knowledge;
- the capability of certain processes;
- the probability that certain events that are outside our control will or will not happen (weather conditions, traffic congestion, mood of the people, etc.).

See also **quality objectives**.

Cross-functional team

Meaning

A cross-functional team is a team of people from different functions. A cross-functional team might comprise people from sales, design, quality assurance and customer service functions.

ISO 9000 requirements and recommendations

- Annex A of ISO 9004, in the context of self-assessment, suggests that an approach would be to have a cross-functional group of people perform self-assessment on all or part of the quality management system.
- Annex B of ISO 9004 advises that breakthrough projects are usually carried out by cross-functional teams outside routine operations.

Application

Where a problem requires for its resolution, the combined inputs from personnel with different skills and competences, the team may be classed as a cross-functional team or a multidisciplinary team. 'Cross-functional' implies people from different functions regardless of competence. 'Multidisciplinary' implies people of different disciplines regardless of functions. For example, you could form a multidisciplinary team from one department simply by bringing together a manager, a personal assistant, an engineer and a technician. Conversely, a cross-functional team could bring together all the administrative staff from all functions – a single discipline team that is multifunctional.

The labels can, therefore, be misleading. Calling a team 'cross-functional' or 'multi-disciplinary' does not convey what is required when one needs a team that is *both* cross-functional and multidisciplinary.

One of the problems with such teams is that the people come together for a meeting to work on a problem but then return to their offices and get on with what they were doing before they left. Locating people in offices appropriate to their function or discipline does have these disadvantages, which is why it is often more effective to locate people according to the primary process or the project they work in or on. Locating planners, administrators, engineers, technicians, operators and inspectors whose work is dedicated to the production of a particular product is more likely to result in building an effective process team that actually implements decisions made in a team meeting. This is not always practical, as people often work on several products/projects where the centre of operations is in different locations.

Culture and climate

If we ask people to describe what it is like to work for a particular organization, they often reply in terms of their feelings and emotions, which are their perceptions of the essential atmosphere in the organization. This atmosphere is encompassed by two concepts – culture and climate.

Culture evolves and can usually be traced back to the organization's founder. The founder gathers around people of like mind and values, and these become the role models for new entrants. Culture has a strong influence on people's behaviour but is not easily changed. It is an invisible force that consists of deeply held beliefs, values and assumptions that are so ingrained in the fabric of the organization that many people might not be conscious that they hold them.

Climate is allied to culture and, although people experience both, climate tends to be something of which there is more awareness. Culture provides a code of conduct that defines acceptable behaviour, whereas climate tends to result in a set of conditions to which people react. Culture is more permanent, whereas climate is temporary and is thought of as a phase the organization passes through. In this context, therefore, the work environment will be affected by a change in the organizational climate. Several external forces cause changes in the climate, such as economic factors, political factors and market factors. These can result in feelings of optimism or pessimism, security or insecurity, complacency or anxiety.

Cultural and climatic factors influence the behaviour of people in the work environment. It is, therefore, important to be aware of those factors that lead to poor performance and employee dissatisfaction and, wherever possible, change them.

Customer

ISO 9000 defines a customer as an organization or person that receives a product or service and includes purchaser, consumer, client, end user, retailer or beneficiary.

Customers are **stakeholders**: they have entered into a commitment in return for some benefits that possession of a product or experience of a service may bring. Customers demand, request or otherwise place an organization under a **commitment**, implying that there is no such thing as an **internal customer**.

The customer is often thought of as the person who buys a product or service but, in the above definition, this is a customer who is a purchaser. The end user may not buy the product but is the person for whom the product or service is produced.

ISO 9000 is primarily produced for business-to-business relationships rather than business-to-consumer relationships. In manufacturing this is more the case as it is with services. Often in a service delivery transaction, the party receiving the service is a consumer.

Customer communication

Meaning

Customer communication is the means used to enable customers to interact with the organization on any matters about which they need to be informed.

ISO 9000 requirements and recommendations

- Clause 7.2.3 of ISO 9001 requires the organization to determine and implement effective arrangements for communication with the customer in relation to product information, enquiries, contracts or order handling, contracts or order amendments and customer feedback, including customer complaints.
- Clause 7.2 of ISO 9004 recommends that management should ensure that the organization has defined mutually acceptable processes for communicating effectively and efficiently with its customers and other interested parties.

Application

The customer communication process should include the following subprocesses:

- A product and service promotion process that ensures information accuracy and compatibility.
- An enquiry conversion process that converts enquiries into sales with the result that both parties are completely satisfied with the transaction.

- An order-processing process that ensures both parties are in no doubt as to the expectations before work commences.
- An order amendment process that honours the commitment and maintains the expectations expressed with the original order.
- A customer feedback process that captures opportunities for improvement and encouragement, honours **commitments** and preserves customer relationships.

Customer complaints

Meaning

A customer complaint is any adverse report (verbal or written) received by an organization from a customer.

ISO 9000 requirements and recommendations

- Clause 7.2.3 of ISO 9001 requires the organization to determine and implement effective arrangements for **communication with the customer** in relation to **customer feedback** including customer complaints.
- Clause 8.5.2 of ISO 9001 requires a documented procedure to be established to define requirements for reviewing nonconformities (including customer complaints).
- Clause 3.1.4 of ISO 9000 advises that customer complaints are a common indicator of low customer satisfaction but their absence does not necessarily imply high customer satisfaction.
- Clause 8.2.1.2 of ISO 9004 suggests that sources of information on customer satisfaction include customer complaints.
- Clause 8.5.2 of ISO 9004 suggests that sources of information for corrective action consideration include customer complaints.

Application

The complaint-handling process should cover the following aspects to be effective:

1 A definition of when a message from a customer can be classified as a complaint.
2 The method of capturing the customer complaints from all interface channels with the customer.
3 The behaviour expected from those on the receiving end of the complaint.
4 The registration of complaints in order that you can account for them and monitor progress.
5 A form on which to record details of the complaint, the date, customer name, etc.
6 A method for acknowledging the complaint in order that the customer knows you care.
7 A method for investigating the nature and cause of the complaint.
8 A method for replacing product, repeating the service or compensating the customer.
9 A link with other processes to trigger improvements that will prevent a recurrence of the complaint.

Customer expectations

Customer expectations are implied needs or requirements. They have not been requested because we take them for granted – we regard them to be understood within our particular society as the accepted norm. They may be things to which we are accustomed, based on fashion, style, trends or previous experience. One, therefore, expects sales staff to be polite and courteous, electronic products to be safe and reliable, policemen to be honest, coffee to be hot, etc.

Customer feedback

Meaning

Customer feedback is any comment on the organization's performance provided by a customer.

ISO 9000 requirements and recommendations

- Clause 5.6.2 of ISO 9001 requires the input to management review to include information on customer feedback.
- Clause 7.2.3 of ISO 9001 requires the organization to determine and implement effective arrangements for communication with the customer in relation to customer feedback.

Application

Customer feedback should be used to establish whether customer needs are being satisfied. You can determine this by providing the evidence of customer complaints, market share statistics, competitor statistics, warranty claims, customer satisfaction surveys, etc. Current performance from customer feedback should compare the results with the quality objectives you have set for customer needs and expectations.

Improvement opportunities relative to customer feedback may cover:

- The extent to which products and services satisfy customer needs and expectations.
- The adequacy of the means used to assess customer satisfaction and collect data.
- The need to develop new or enhanced products or services.
- The need to explore new markets or obtain more accurate data of current markets.

The **compliment** handling process should cover the following:

- A definition of when a message from a customer can be classified as a compliment.
- A method of capturing the compliments from all interface channels with the customer.
- The behaviour expected from those on the receiving end of the compliment.
- The registration of compliments in order that you can account for those you can use in your promotional literature.
- A method for keeping staff informed of the compliments made by customers.
- A method of rewarding staff when compliments result in further business.

Customer focus

Customer focus is one of the eight quality management principles used as a basis for developing ISO 9000. The principle is expressed as 'Organizations depend on their customers and therefore should understand current and future customer needs, should meet **customer requirements** and strive to exceed **customer expectations**'.

All organizations have customers. They exist to create and retain satisfied customers. Those that do not do so, fail to survive. It is, therefore, essential for the survival of an organization that it determines and meets customer requirements.

An organization applying the customer focus principle would be one in which people:

- understood customer needs and expectations;
- balanced the needs and expectations of all interested parties;
- communicated these needs and expectations throughout the organization;
- had the knowledge, skills and resources required to satisfy the organization's customers;
- measured customer satisfaction and acted on results;
- managed customer relationships;
- could relate their goals and targets directly to customer needs and expectations; and
- acted upon the results of customer satisfaction measurements.

Customer needs

Customer needs are essential for survival, to maintain certain standards, or essential for products and services to fulfil the purpose for which they have been acquired.

By focusing on benefits resulting from products and services, needs can be converted into wants such that a need for food may be converted into a want for a particular brand of chocolate. This is the role of marketing – converting needs into wants so that customers want your products in preference to your competitors' products.

Sometimes the *want* is not essential but, the higher up the hierarchy of needs we go, the more a *want* becomes essential to maintain our social standing, esteem or to realize our personal goals. Our requirements may, therefore, include such wants – what we would like to have but which are not essential for survival.

Customer property

Meaning

Customer property is any property owned or provided by the customer. The product being supplied may have been produced by a competitor, by the customer or even by your own firm under a different contract or sales agreement.

Customer property may be supplied:

- For use in a sales transaction, such as credit card details and personal information.
- For use on a contract, in order to design or produce the product, such as design information, software or test equipment.
- For use in order to ship the product, such as packaging and labels.
- For incorporation into a product to be supplied, such as a gyroscope that is to be fitted into a missile.

ISO 9000 requirements and recommendations

Clause 7.5.4 of ISO 9001 requires the organization to:

- Exercise care with customer property while it is under the organization's control or being used by the organization.
- Identify, verify, protect and safeguard customer property provided for use or incorporation into the product.
- Report to the customer if any customer property is lost, damaged or otherwise found to be unsuitable for use.

Application

For customer property that is in the form of hardware and software product, which is used on your own premises, you should maintain a register containing details of customer property that will enable it to be located on request by the customer.

For customer property that is in the form of credit card details and other personal information, you should provide secure storage that will protect the information against unauthorized use and inadvertent loss. If the data are stored electronically, you will need to comply with any relevant data protection laws.

Customer requirements

Meaning

In the context of ISO 9000, a customer requirement is a need or expectation of a customer that is stated, customarily implied or obligatory.

ISO 9000 requirements and recommendations

- Clause 5.2 of ISO 9001 requires top management to ensure that customer requirements are determined and are met with the aim of enhancing customer satisfaction.
- Clause 5.5.2 of ISO 9001 requires the appointed member of management to have responsibility and authority for ensuring the promotion of **awareness** of customer requirements.

Application

In order to determine customer needs and expectations you need to know:

- Who your customers are – they may not be simply those that purchase your products (see **customer**).
- Where your customers are located – geography affects needs.
- What your customers buy – do they buy luxury, comfort, security, health, happiness, status or simply utility?
- What the customers value – which characteristic is more important than others: safety, reliability, integrity, personal attention, speed, durability, etc.?
- Which of the customer's wants are not adequately satisfied – 'It's a status symbol but very unreliable', 'It's reliable but old-fashioned'.

The answers to the above questions will enable marketing objectives to be established for:

- existing products and services in present markets;
- abandonment of obsolete products, services and markets;
- new products and services for existing markets/new markets;
- service standards and service performance;
- product standards and product performance.

The results of market research will be a mixture of things. It will identify:

- new potential customers for existing products and services;
- new potential markets;
- opportunities for which no technology exists;

- opportunities for which no product or service solution exists;
- enhancements to existing products and services.

The organization needs to decide which of these to pursue and this requires a marketing process that involves all the interested parties. It is also not sufficient to simply capture what customers say they want.

Customer satisfaction

Meaning

By combining definitions of the terms 'customer satisfaction' and 'requirement', ISO 9000 defines customer satisfaction as 'the customer's perception of the degree to which the customer's stated or implied needs or expectations have been fulfilled'.

Information relating to customer perception is any meaningful data from which a judgement can be made about customer satisfaction and would include compliments, complaints, sales statistics, survey results, etc.

ISO 9000 requirements and recommendations

- Clause 1.1 of ISO 9001 states that the Standard specifies requirements for a quality management system where an organization aims to enhance customer satisfaction.
- Clause 5.2 of ISO 9001 requires top management to ensure that customer requirements are determined and are met with the aim of enhancing customer satisfaction.
- Clause 6.1 of ISO 9001 requires the organization to determine and provide the resources needed to enhance customer satisfaction.
- Clause 8.2.1 of ISO 9001 requires the organization to monitor information relating to customer satisfaction as one of the measurements of the performance of the quality management system.
- Clause 8.4 of ISO 9001 requires the analysis of data to provide information relating to customer satisfaction.

Application

In order to satisfy customers, you have to go beyond the stated requirements. Customers are people and people differ in their perceptions as to whether the transaction has been satisfactory. The term 'perception' is used because 'satisfaction' is a subjective and human condition (unlike 'acceptance', which is based on objective evidence). Customers may accept a product but not be wholly satisfied with it or the service they have received. Whether or not you have done your utmost to please the customer, if the customer's perception is that you have not met their expectations, he or she will not be satisfied.

There are several ways of monitoring information relating to customer perceptions, ranging from unsolicited information to customer focus meetings.

- Repeat orders. The number of repeat orders or the period over which customers remain loyal.
- Competition. Monitoring what the competition is up to is an indicator of your success or failure.
- Referrals. When you win a new customer, find out why they chose your organization in preference to others.
- Demand. Monitoring the demand for your products and services relative to the predicted demand is also an indicator of success or failure to satisfy customers.

- Effects of product transition. When you launch a new product or service, do you retain your customers or do they take the opportunity to go elsewhere?
- **Customer surveys** – there is the impersonal form and the personal form. The impersonal form relies on responses to questionnaires and seeks to establish customer opinion on a number of topics. The personal form of survey is conducted through interview.
- Focus meetings. A personal form of obtaining information on customer satisfaction is to arrange to meet with your customer and seek opinions from the people within the customer's organization.
- **Customer complaints**. Look at the overall number of complaints, the upward or downward trends, and the distribution of complaints by type of customer, location and nature of complaint.
- **Compliments**. Compliments are harder to monitor because they can vary from a passing remark during a sales transaction to a formal letter.

Customer surveys

Meaning

A customer survey is a means of obtaining information from customers about how they perceive your products and services.

ISO 9000 requirements and recommendations

There is no requirement in ISO 9000 for customer surveys or questionnaires, but these are tools that can be used to determine customer satisfaction levels.

Application

When designing a survey or questionnaire:

- Do not ask more than 50 questions.
- Probe low satisfaction scores rather than high satisfaction scores, unless there are no low scores.
- Spread the questions over four pages (four sides), as it looks more balanced and gets a higher response rate.
- Provide instructions on the first page.
- Do not use complex questions that require two or more answers.
- Always seek relative measures of importance/unimportance, as it reflects what is of value to customers, e.g. on a scale of 1–10.
- Low satisfaction with a characteristic of low importance is not as critical as low satisfaction with a characteristic of high importance.
- Separate questions on satisfaction from questions of importance and position questions on satisfaction before questions on importance.
- Always place questions concerning the interviewee on the last page.
- Avoid jargon and acronyms.
- Ratings such as 'excellent', 'good', 'average' and 'poor' tend to bias the answers.
- Numerical scales of 1–10 are more discriminating and are better for data analysis.

Data

Meaning

The term 'data' means information that is organized in a form suitable for manual or computer analysis.

ISO 9000 requirements and recommendations

- Clause 8.1 of ISO 9001 requires the organization to determine, collect and analyse appropriate data to demonstrate the suitability and effectiveness of the quality management system and to evaluate where continual improvement of the quality management system can be made.
- Clause 6.5 of ISO 9004 recommends that management should treat data as a fundamental resource for conversion to information and the continual development of an organization's knowledge, which is essential for making factual decisions and can stimulate innovation.

Application

The management system generates a lot of data and processes need to be put in place that govern data generation, **collection**, transmission, **analysis** and **security**.

In some cases the data may be confidential or governed by data protection laws. Data transmission by electronic means may require encryption to prevent unauthorized use. Data may need to be protected from unauthorized access by electronic means by providing *firewalls* or by manual means by providing passwords.

Demonstrate

Meaning

Demonstrate means to prove by reasoning, objective evidence, experiment or practical application.

ISO 9000 requirements and recommendations

- Clause 1.1 of ISO 9001 states that the Standard specifies requirements for a quality management system where an organization needs to demonstrate its ability to consistently provide product that meets customer and applicable regulatory requirements.

- Clause 7.5.2 of ISO 9001 requires process validation to demonstrate the ability of processes to achieve planned results.
- Clause 8.1 of ISO 9001 requires the organization to plan and implement the monitoring, measurement, analysis and improvement processes needed to demonstrate conformity of the product.
- Clause 8.2.3 of ISO 9001 requires the organization to apply suitable methods, which demonstrate the ability of the processes to achieve planned results.
- Clause 8.3 of ISO 9001 requires nonconforming product to be subject to re-verification to demonstrate conformity to the requirements when it is corrected.
- Clause 8.4 of ISO 9001 requires the organization to determine, collect and analyse appropriate data to demonstrate the suitability and effectiveness of the quality management system.

Application

The need to demonstrate anything arises from the market in which the organization operates. ISO 9000 was primarily produced for a business-to-business (B2B) relationship rather than a business-to-consumer (B2C) relationship. In a B2B situation, the customer is another business and may require suppliers to demonstrate their ability to meet customer requirements. In a B2C relationship, the consumer does not require demonstration but expects the supplier to honour its **commitments**. Therefore, meeting requirements and demonstrating that requirements have been met have the same intent but may require a different type of management system. Where demonstration is required, the supplier may have a choice of how compliance is demonstrated.

If compliance can be demonstrated by observation, no documentary evidence may be needed. However, if the customer or regulator cannot witness the activities (which is more often the case), some documentary evidence is necessary. The evidence may be in the form of paper records, computer records, video, film or audio records.

You need to draw a distinction between evidence needed for control, improvement and demonstration purposes. Often the three are the same but there are occasions when they are different. Records needed for improvement purposes may not be necessary for control purposes, e.g. charts of last week's production are no longer needed for controlling next week's production, but are needed to analyse trends and identify opportunities for improvement. No records may be needed for control purposes but records may be needed to demonstrate continued compliance with regulations.

This distinction has brought about a plethora of documentation that only serves one purpose – that of demonstrating compliance with ISO 9000 or other standards. Some of the documentation does not have any other purpose. However, the danger lies in the statement in ISO 9001 clause 4.2.1 where it requires documents needed by the organization to ensure the effective planning, operation and control of its processes. This implies that, if the documentation is not needed for effective planning, operation and control of its processes, there is necessity to produce it. If an operation could be closed down by a regulator through a lack of documentary evidence, such documentation would be needed for legal operation of the process concerned.

If this is an issue, you should assess all your documentation and classify it as essential (E), mandatory (M), or both essential and mandatory (E&M). In this way, you will be able to compare how much documentation is maintained simply to comply with standards and regulations as opposed to that which is necessary to run the business!

Department

A department is a unit of an organization that may perform one or more functions. Units of organization regardless of their names are also referred to as **functions** but this can be an incorrect use of the term because a particular department may not perform all the activities encompassed by a function. It equally may perform activities that serve other functions.

Functions may also be executed by more than one department. For example, the design function may be executed by a systems engineering department, an electronic design department and a mechanical engineering department. Tooling design and plant design may also be executed by different departments. Similarly the marketing function may be executed by several departments, each performing a role in the **marketing process**.

Design

Design is a process of originating a conceptual solution to a requirement and expressing it in a form from which a product may be produced or a service delivered.

Design and development

Meaning

Design and development is a process or two processes depending on the objective. Design creates the conceptual solution and development transforms the solution into a fully working model that performs exactly as intended.

Development can also mean taking an existing design or concept and making it better, enhancing it, modifying it so as to produce something new. Ideas are not designed but are developed from basic concepts. Similarly, a capability is not designed but is developed. The difference is one of originality. Although one might say that laser printers have developed over the years, each one is designed to fulfil a unique requirement and then developed so as to meet the changing needs of the market. Architects and civil engineers design structures rather than develop them, whereas automotive engineers design a motor car and develop its capability. Development nearly always involves trials, learning from observations and improving the design as a result.

Control of design and development does not mean controlling the creativity of the designers – it means controlling the process through which new or modified designs are produced so that the resultant design is one that truly reflects customer needs.

ISO 9000 requirements and recommendations

Clause 7.3.1 of ISO 9001 requires the organization to plan and control the design and development of product.

Application

To control any design activity, there are ten primary steps you need to take in the design and development process:

1 Establish the customer needs.
2 Convert the customer needs into a definitive specification of the requirements.
3 Plan for meeting the requirements.
4 Organize resources and materials for meeting the requirements.

5 Conduct a feasibility study to discover whether accomplishment of the requirements is feasible.
6 Conduct a project definition study to discover which of the many possible solutions will be the most suitable.
7 Develop a specification that details all the features and characteristics of the product or service.
8 Produce a prototype or model of the proposed design.
9 Conduct extensive trials to discover whether the product or service that has been developed meets the design requirements and customer needs.
10 Feed data back into the design and repeat the process until the product or service is proven to be fit for the task.

Design changes

Meaning

Design changes are simply changes to the design and can occur at any stage in the design process from the stage at which the requirement is agreed to the final certification that the design is proven and, subsequently, at any time in the life cycle of the design. Following design certification, i.e. when all **design verification** has been completed and the product launched into production, changes to the product to incorporate design changes are generally classed as 'modifications'.

Changes to design documents are not design changes unless the characteristics of the product are altered. Changes in the presentation of design information or to the system of measurement (Imperial units to metric units) are not design or development changes.

ISO 9000 requirements and recommendations

Clause 7.3.7 of ISO 9001 requires design and development changes to be identified, reviewed, verified and validated, as appropriate, and approved before implementation and records maintained.

Application

You need to control design changes to permit desirable changes to be made and to prohibit undesirable changes from being made. Change control during the design process is a good method of controlling costs and timescales because, once the design process has commenced, every change will cost time and effort to implement, not only to the areas of the design directly affected but any interfacing areas on which design may also have commenced.

The design change control process consists of a number of elements:

1 A mechanism for establishing the design baseline.
2 A design authority to whom all requests of changes are to be submitted.
3 A means of requesting a design change and the reason for it.
4 A means of transmitting the request for change to the design authority for evaluation.
5 A means of evaluating the proposed design change for need, importance and impact.
6 A change proposal approval/rejection stage.
7 Conventions to be used in identifying the issue status of design documents during development and following design certification.

8 A stage for approval or rejection of the new design.

9 A mechanism for notifying those concerned of the approved design change, the point of embodiment, how to deal with existing product or service and how to deal with new product or service.

10 A means of recording the actions taken at each stage in the process so that the integrity of the change can be verified.

Design inputs

Meaning

The design inputs are the requirements governing the design of the intended product. They include all the requirements determined from an analysis of customer and regulatory requirements and the organization's requirements.

ISO 9000 requirements and recommendations

Clause 7.3.2 of ISO 9001 requires inputs relating to product requirements to be determined and records maintained.

Application

To identify design input requirements you need to identify:

- The purpose of the product or service.
- The conditions under which it will be used, stored and transported.
- The skills and category of those who will use and maintain the product or service.
- The countries to which it will be sold and the related regulations governing sale and use of products.
- The special features and performance characteristics which the customer requires the product or service to exhibit.
- The constraints in terms of timescale, operating environment, cost, size, weight or other factors.
- The standards with which the product or service needs to comply.
- The products or service with which it will directly and indirectly interface, and their features and characteristics.
- The documentation required of the design output necessary to manufacture, procure, inspect, test, install, operate and maintain a product or service.

Design outputs

Meaning

Design output is the product of the design process and hence will comprise information and/ or models and specimens that describe the design in all its detail, the calculations, assumptions and the rationale for the chosen solution. It is not simply the specifications or drawings because should the design need to be changed, the designer may need to revisit the design data to modify parameters and assumptions.

ISO 9000 requirements and recommendations

Clause 7.3.3 of ISO 9001 requires the outputs of design and development to be provided in a form that enables verification against the design and development input and shall be approved prior to release.

Application

The design input requirements should have been expressed in a way that would allow a number of possible solutions. The design output requirements should, therefore, be expressed as all the inherent features and characteristics of the design that reflect a product that will satisfy these requirements. Hence, it should fulfil the stated or implied needs, i.e. be fit for purpose.

In order to accomplish this a number of actions are required:

1 Determine the design output requirements before commencing design.
2 Identify who will produce the design output information.
3 Ensure design output requirements are conveyed to those concerned.
4 Establish standards and procedures to govern the format and content of design output documents.
5 Establish a process for producing, reviewing and approving design output information.
6 Determine the types of documents that will comprise the total design output information.
7 Determine the calculations and analyses that are needed to verify that the design output information reflects a product that meets the input requirements.
8 Determine the checks to be performed to verify that the design information reflects a product that can be manufactured, inspected, tested, installed and serviced.
9 Decide when design output checks will be performed.
10 Indicate in the design information the characteristics that are critical to success.
11 Determine how release of design information is to be denoted following its approval.

Design planning

Meaning

Planning the design and development of a product means determining the design objectives and the design strategy, the design stages, timescales, costs, resources and responsibilities needed to accomplish them. Sometimes the activity of design itself is considered to be a planning activity, but what is being planned is not the design but the product.

ISO 9000 requirements and recommendations

Clause 7.3.1 of ISO 9001 requires the organization to plan and control the design and development of the product.

Application

Design and development plans should include:

1 The design requirements.
2 The design and development programme showing activities against time.
3 The work packages and names of those who will execute them.

4 The work breakdown structure showing the relationship between all the parcels of work.
5 The reviews to be held for authorizing work to proceed from stage to stage.
6 The resources in terms of finance, manpower and facilities.
7 The risks to success and the plans to minimize them.
8 The controls that will be exercised to keep the design on course.

Design review

Meaning

A design **review** is a formal documented and systematic critical study of a design by people other than the designer. The purpose of the review is to determine whether the proposed design solution is compliant with the design requirement and whether design should continue or should be changed before proceeding to the next phase.

ISO 9000 defines a review as an activity undertaken to determine the suitability, adequacy and effectiveness of the subject matter to achieve established objectives. This is the way the term should be interpreted in the context of ISO 9000. When the term 'review' is used in another context, it simply means to have another look at something.

Suitability means 'Has an appropriate design solution been developed?'. Adequacy means 'Does the design solution meet all the design requirements?'. Effectiveness means 'Have we got the right design objective?'. Design reviews are, therefore, *not* document reviews.

Systematic reviews are those that cover the complete design from the high level down to the smallest component and all the associated requirements in a logical manner.

ISO 9000 requirements and recommendations

Clause 7.3.4 of ISO 9001 requires the organization to perform systematic reviews of design and development in accordance with planned arrangements at suitable stages to evaluate the ability of the results of the design and development to meet requirements.

Application

The review has to be stage by stage, methodical with purpose. Systematic reviews probe the design solution and the interfaces between all components for design weaknesses and delve into the detail to explore how requirements are fulfilled.

Typical stages when design reviews are undertaken include the following.

- *Design requirement review.* A review performed prior to commencing design to establish that the design requirements can be met and reflect the needs of the customer before commencement of design.
- *Conceptual design review.* A review performed after sketching out a conceptual solution to establish that the design concept fulfils the requirements before project definition commences.
- *Preliminary design review.* A review performed after completing the functional design to establish that all risks have been resolved and development specifications have been produced for each sub-element of the product/service before detail design commences.
- *Critical design review.* A review performed after detailing all components to establish that the detail design for each sub-element of the product/service complies with its development specification, and that product specifications have been produced before manufacture of the prototypes.

- *Qualification readiness review.* A review performed after design verification to establish the configuration of the baseline design and readiness for qualification before commencement of design validation.
- *Final design review.* A review performed after design verification and validation to establish that the design fulfils the requirements of its development specification before preparation for its production.

To conduct an effective design review process you should:

- Distribute input data to the review team well in advance of the time when a decision on the design has to be made.
- Not assume you can review a complete design at a meeting. A design review is not a meeting, it is a critical review of a design and requires concentration, analysis, investigation, research and other techniques to produce a valid result.
- Find flaws in the design before they become too costly to correct.
- Utilize experiences of previous designs.
- Use checklists developed from experience and research to aid the evaluation of designs.
- Ensure the review team has a collective competency greater than that of the designer of the design being reviewed.
- Ensure representation at each review is appropriate to the design stage being reviewed.
- Appoint a leader of the review team who is responsible for placing the development requirement.
- Ensure the review leader makes the decision as to whether the design should proceed to the next phase based on the evidence substantiated by the review team.
- Ensure the review report has the agreement of the full review team.

Design validation

Meaning

ISO 9000 defines **validation** as confirmation through the provision of **objective evidence** that requirements for a specific intended use or application have been fulfilled.

Specified requirements are often an imperfect definition of needs and expectations and, therefore, to overcome inadequacies in the manner in which requirements can be specified, the resultant design needs to be validated against intended use or application.

Design validation is a process of evaluating a design to establish that it fulfils the intended use requirements. It goes further than design verification in that validation tests and trials may stress the product of such a design beyond operating conditions in order to establish design margins of safety and performance. Design validation can also be performed on mature designs in order to establish whether they will fulfil different user requirements to the original design input requirements. (See also **validation and verification**.)

ISO 9000 requirements and recommendations

Clause 7.3.6 of ISO 9001 requires the organization to perform design and development validation in accordance with planned arrangements.

Application

The design validation process consists of a number of elements. (The term 'trials' is used for validation activities in contrast to tests for verification activities.)

1 Plan for validation as part of your product development planning.
2 Establish how user characteristics are to be demonstrated (which models of what standard will be used for validating which requirements).
3 Establish the model philosophy for carrying out validation trials.
4 Prepare detailed plans for specific trials that define the sequence of trials, the responsibilities for their conduct, the location of the trials and trials procedures to be used.
5 Produce specifications that define the features and characteristics that are to be verified for design qualification and acceptance.
6 Produce procedures that describe how the validation trials specified in the validation specification are to be conducted, together with the tools and test equipment to be used and the data to be recorded.
7 Provide demonstration models that are fully representative of those that will be supplied to customers for the features being validated.
8 Organize the resources necessary to carry out the trials.
9 Acquire the equipment, facilities, sites, etc., for carrying out the trials.
10 Ensure all measuring equipment is within calibration during the trials.
11 Ensure the trial sample has successfully passed all planned in-process and assembly inspections and tests prior to commencing validation trials.
12 Record the configuration of the product prior to and subsequent to the trials in terms of its design standard, deviations, nonconformances and design changes.
13 Do not permit modifications without prior authorization.
14 Conduct pre-trial reviews to establish the validation baseline and confirm operational readiness for validation.
15 Conduct the trials in accordance with the approved documentation.
16 Record all the results, including any on-site changes to parameters, nonconformities and conditions under which the test were performed.
17 Deviations should be recorded, remedial action taken and the product subject to re-verification prior to continuing with the trials.
18 Conduct post-trial reviews to establish that the objectives have been met and that sufficient objective evidence has been obtained to **demonstrate** that the product fulfils the product requirements.
19 Do not use previous models unless you know their history and you are in possession of the records.
20 Feedback all modifications into the design process so that future models can be built to the same standard.

Design verification

Meaning

ISO 9000 defines **verification** as confirmation, through the provision of **objective evidence** that specified requirements have been fulfilled.

There are two types of verification: those verification activities performed during design and on the component parts to verify conformance to specification; and those verification activities performed on the completed design to verify performance against the design input. When designing a system, there should be design requirements for each subsystem, each item of equipment and each unit, and so on down to the component and raw-material level. Each of these design requirements represents acceptance criteria for verifying the design output of each stage. Verification may take the form of a document review, laboratory tests, alternative calculations, similarity analyses or tests and demonstrations on representative samples, prototypes, etc. that the design stage output meets the design stage input requirements. In all these cases, the purpose is to prove that the design is right, i.e. it meets the requirements.

ISO 9000 requirements and recommendations

Clause 7.3.5 of ISO 9001 requires the organization to perform design and development verification in accordance with planned arrangements to ensure that design and development outputs meet the design and development input requirements.

Application

The design verification process consists of a number of elements. Many of the elements addressed under **design validation** also apply.

1 Identify the requirements for which verification is required.
2 Establish the method of verification of each requirement (test, inspection, analysis, simulation, demonstration or simply verification of records).
3 Establish the objectives of verification. You may need several plans covering different aspects of the requirements.
4 Define the specifications and procedures to be employed for determining that each requirement has been achieved.
5 Define the stages in the development phase at which verification can most economically be carried out.
6 Identify the various models that will be used to demonstrate achievement of design requirements. Some models may be simple space models, and others may be of laboratory standard or production standard, depending on the need.
7 Do not start making prototypes until the interface dimensions have been confirmed.
8 Define the product design standard that is being verified.
9 Record the design documentation status used in the performance of calculations and analyses.
10 Define the verification activities that are to be performed to verify the design and those which need to be performed on every product in production as a means of ensuring that the qualified design standard has been maintained.
11 Define the test equipment, support equipment and facilities needed to carry out the verification activities.
12 Define the timescales for the verification activities in the sequence in which the activities are to be carried out.
13 Identify the venue for the verification activities.
14 Identify the organization responsible for conducting each of the verification activities.
15 Identify the controls to be exercised over the verification process. Provision should also be included for dealing with failures, their remedy, investigation and action on design modifications.
16 Do not start pre-production until the design has been functionally proven.
17 Decide on the methods to be employed to make the transition from development to pre-production, and from pre-production to production.

Determining requirements

Meaning

A requirement is a need or expectation that is stated, generally implied or obligatory. The determination of requirements is, therefore, not simply looking at what the customer has stated, but involves the exploration of needs, expectations and regulations to discover every condition that may impact the inherent characteristics of the outcome.

ISO 9000 requirements and recommendations

- Clause 7.2.1a of ISO 9001 requires the organization to determine requirements specified by the customer including requirements for delivery and post-delivery.
- Clause 7.2.1b of ISO 9001 requires the organization to determine requirements not stated by the customer but necessary for specified or intended use, where known.
- Clause 7.2.1c of ISO 9001 requires the organization to determine statutory and regulatory requirements related to the product.
- Clause 7.2.1a of ISO 9001 requires the organization to determine any additional requirements related to the product.

Application

The determination of requirements relating to the product should be approached from two perspectives: from the viewpoint of an identified market need; and from the viewpoint of a specific contract or order. Before you decide what design, production or service delivery capability you need, you should establish what customers in your segment of the market are looking for: what unsatisfied needs they have, and what the competition provides. This will enable you to develop a capability that responds to the needs of the market. On receipt of specific enquiries, orders or contracts, you should determine exactly what the customer requires, needs, expects or wants. This will enable you to match your capability to customer needs.

The organization, and not the customer, is responsible for determining requirements. The customer may not know what you need to know to design or produce the product or supply the service and, therefore, you have to find out by asking pertinent questions.

You need to ensure that:

- There is a clear definition of the purpose of the product or service you are being contracted to supply.
- The conditions of use are clearly specified.
- The national and international regulations, laws and standards are determined that apply to the product, its production, and its export and use.
- The requirements are specified in terms of the features and characteristics that will make the product or service fit for its intended purpose.
- The interface requirements are specified in terms that will ensure compatibility and interchangeability.
- The quantity, price and delivery are specified.
- The contractual requirements are specified including: warranty, payment conditions, acceptance conditions, customer supplied material, financial liability, legal matters, penalties, subcontracting, licences and design rights.
- The management requirements are specified, such as points of contact, programme plans, work breakdown structure, progress reporting, meetings, reviews and interfaces.

- The quality assurance requirements are specified, such as quality system standards, quality plans, reports, customer surveillance and concessions.

Document approval

Meaning

By subjecting documentation to an approval process prior to release, you can ensure that the documents in use have been judged by authorized personnel and found fit for purpose. Such a practice will also ensure that no unapproved documents are in circulation, thereby preventing errors from the use of invalid documents.

ISO 9000 requirements and recommendations

Clause 4.2.3 of ISO 9001 requires a documented procedure to be established to define the controls needed to approve documents for adequacy prior to issue.

Application

The document approval process should address the following aspects:

- Each document should have a specific purpose or objective (the reason for which it has been produced).
- **Acceptance criteria** should be defined to enable approval authorities to make decisions on the basis of fact.
- Approval authorities should be defined.
- Provide a means by which **controlled documents** are submitted to the nominated approval authorities prior to release for use.
- Provide a means for the approval authorities to denote approval or rejection of the document that is visible to users.

Document approval can be denoted by signatures but, if the document is released through a controlled process in which only approved documents are accessible for use, signatures are unnecessary.

Document change request

Meaning

A document change request is a vehicle for transmitting a request for change to the authority responsible for maintaining a document.

ISO 9000 requirements and recommendations

ISO 9000 does not address document change requests.

Application

Change requests need to specify:

- The document title, issue and date.
- The originator of the change request (who is proposing the change, his/her location or department).

- The reason for change (why the change is necessary).
- What needs to be changed (which paragraph, section, etc. is affected and what text should be deleted).
- The changes in text required, where known (the text which is to be inserted or deleted).

Document control

Meaning

Documents are *information carriers* – document control means control of the information and the medium by which it is conveyed (paper, film or computer disk).

Controlling information means regulating the development, approval, issue, change, distribution, maintenance, use, storage, security, obsolescence or disposal of information. You do not need to exercise control over each of these elements for a document to be designated as a controlled document. Controlling documents may be limited to controlling their revision. On the other hand, you cannot control the revision of national standards but you can control their use, storage, obsolescence, etc. Even memoranda can become **controlled documents**, if you impose a security classification upon them.

ISO 9000 requirements and recommendations

Clause 4.2.3 of ISO 9001 requires documents required by the quality management system to be controlled.

Application

The aspects you should cover in your document control process are as follows:

- Planning new documents – funding, prior authorization, establishing need, etc.
- Preparation of documents – who prepares them, how they are drafted, conventions for text, diagrams, forms, etc.
- Standards for the format and content of documents, forms and diagrams.
- **Document identification** conventions.
- Issue notation, draft issues, post-approval issues.
- Dating conventions – date of issue, date of approval or date of distribution.
- **Document review** – who reviews them and what evidence is retained.
- **Document approval** – who approves them and how approval is denoted.
- Document proving prior to use.
- Printing and publication – who does it and who checks it.
- Distribution of documents – who decides, who does it and who checks it.
- Use of documents – limitations, unauthorized copying and marking.
- Revision of issued documents – requests for revision, who approves the request and who implements the change.
- Denoting changes – revision marks, re-issues, sidelining and underlining.
- Amending copies of issued documents – amendment instructions and amendment status.
- Indexing documents and listing documents by issue status.
- Document maintenance – keeping them current and periodic review.
- Document accessibility inside and outside normal working hours.
- **Document security** – unauthorized changes, copying, disposal, computer viruses, fire and theft.
- Document filing – masters, copies, drafts, and custom binders.

- Document storage, libraries and archives – who controls the location and loan arrangements.
- Document retention and **obsolescence**.

Document identification

Meaning

Document identification (see **identifying document changes**) is assigning a characteristic to a document that renders it unique and retrievable.

ISO 9000 requirements and recommendations

Clause 4.2.3 of ISO 9001 requires the organization to ensure that:

- Changes and the current **revision status** of documents are identified.
- Documents remain legible and readily identifiable.
- Documents of external origin are identified.
- Suitable identification is applied to **obsolete documents**, if they are retained for any purpose.

Application

Three primary means are used for document identification: classification, titles, and identification numbers. Classification divides documents into groups based on their purpose: policies, procedures, records, plans, etc. Titles are acceptable providing there are no two documents with the same title in the same class.

Identification numbers can contain the class of document as well as a serial number to assign a unique identity. Unique identities are more easily achieved with alpha-numeric codes than with titles.

Document review

Meaning

Document review is a review that is carried out at any time following the issue of a document.

ISO 9000 requirements and recommendations

Clause 4.2.3 of ISO 9001 requires the organization to define the controls needed to review documents.

Application

Reviews may be random or periodic. Random reviews are reactive and arise from an error or a change that is either planned or unplanned. Periodic reviews are proactive and could be scheduled once each year to review the policies, processes, products, procedures, specification, etc. for continued suitability. In this way, obsolete documents are removed from the system. However, if the system is being properly maintained, there should be no outdated information available in the user domain. Whenever a new process or a modified process is installed, redundant elements should be disposed of, including documentation and equipment.

Document revision

Meaning

Document revision is a change made to information contained within a document.

ISO 9000 requirements and recommendations

Clause 4.2.3 of ISO 9001 requires the organization to define the controls needed to:

- Update documents as necessary following review.
- Ensure that changes and the current revision status of documents are identified.

Application

It should be possible to establish what has been changed in a document following its revision. When a document is revised, its status changes to signify that it is no longer identical to the original version.

The document change process consists of a number of key stages:

- identification of need;
- request for change;
- permission to change;
- revision of document;
- identifying the change;
- recording the change;
- review of the change;
- approval of the change;
- issue of change instructions;
- issue of revised document.

Document security

Meaning

Document security is concerned with safeguarding documents and the information they contain against loss and unauthorized access, change and transmission.

ISO 9000 requirements and recommendations

Clause 6.5 of ISO 9004 recommends that the organization manages information to ensure appropriate security and confidentiality.

Application

It is not easy to control the distribution of information using physical controls alone. It needs a **culture** of integrity to prevent information from getting into the hands of those who do not have the right to it.

Security measures may include:

- Computer virus controls that prevent incoming viruses entering the information network from telephone lines, radio signals, floppy disks and CDs.
- Password controls for accessing, changing, storing, copying and transmitting information.
- Disaster recovery plans for restoring information lost as a result of computer crash, natural or manmade disaster.

Some organizations prohibit the use of all personal floppy disks and CDs as a means of limiting the sources of attack. A balance has to be attained between security of the information and its accessibility. You may need to consider those who work outside normal working hours and those rare occasions when the troubleshooters are working late, perhaps away from base with their only contact via a computer link.

Controls should ensure that records are not destroyed without prior authorization. Depending on the medium on which data are recorded and the security classification of the data, you may also need to specify the method of disposal.

Documented procedures

Meaning

Documented procedures are **procedures** that are formally laid down in a reproducible medium, such as paper or magnetic disk.

ISO 9000 requirements and recommendations

- Clause 4.2.1 of ISO 9001 requires the quality management system documentation to include documented procedures required by this International Standard.
- Clause 4.2.1 of ISO 9001 requires the organization to establish and maintain a quality manual that includes the documented procedures established for the quality management system, or reference to them.
- Clause 4.2.3 of ISO 9001 requires a documented procedure to be established to define the controls needed to control documents required by the quality management system.
- Clause 4.2.4 of ISO 9001 requires a documented procedure to be established to define the controls needed for the identification, storage, protection, retrieval, retention time and disposition of records.
- Clause 8.2.2 of ISO 9001 requires the responsibilities and requirements for planning and conducting audits, and for reporting results and maintaining records to be defined in a documented procedure.
- Clause 8.3 of ISO 9001 requires the controls and related responsibilities and authorities for dealing with nonconforming product to be defined in a documented procedure.
- Clause 8.5.2 of ISO 9001 requires a documented procedure to be established to define requirements for corrective action.
- Clause 8.3 of ISO 9001 requires a documented procedure to be established to define requirements for preventive action.

Application

Although there are requirements in ISO 9001 for six documented procedures, it is not intended that six separate documents be produced. A procedure can be a single statement, a paragraph or a list of actions. It depends on what is being described and the complexity of the actions required for executing it.

There may be many types of documents, records, nonconformities, audits, corrective actions and preventive actions, each requiring different controls. The procedures needed will vary depending on the nature and complexity of the task, the competence of the personnel and the risks likely to be encountered.

In response to the requirement for processes, do not simply insert a flow chart in your procedures and call them processes. This is not what is meant by **process**.

Effectiveness of the system

Meaning

The effectiveness of a system is the extent to which a system fulfils its purpose.

As the purpose of the quality management system is to enable the organization to achieve its **mission**, goals and **objectives**, continually improving the effectiveness of the management system means continually increasing the ability of the organization to fulfil its mission, goals and objectives. (See also **system effectiveness**.)

ISO 9000 requirements and recommendations

- Clause 4.1 of ISO 9001 requires the organization to improve the effectiveness of the quality management system continually.
- Clause 5.1 of ISO 9001 requires top management to provide evidence of its **commitment** to improving the effectiveness of the quality management system continually.
- Clause 5.3 of ISO 9001 requires top management to ensure that the quality policy includes a commitment to improve the effectiveness of the quality management system continually.
- Clause 5.5.3 of ISO 9001 requires top management to ensure that communication takes place regarding the effectiveness of the quality management system.
- Clause 5.6.1 of ISO 9001 requires top management to review the organization's quality management system, at planned intervals, to ensure its continuing effectiveness.
- Clause 5.6.3 of ISO 9001 requires the output from the management review to include any decisions and actions related to improvement of the effectiveness of the quality management system and its processes.
- Clause 6.1 of ISO 9001 requires the organization to determine and provide the resources needed to improve the effectiveness of the quality management system continually.
- Clause 8.1 of ISO 9001 requires the organization to plan and implement the monitoring, measurement, analysis and improvement processes needed to improve the effectiveness of the quality management system continually.
- Clause 8.4 of ISO 9001 requires the organization to determine, collect and analyse appropriate data to **demonstrate** the suitability and effectiveness of the quality management system.
- Clause 8.5 of ISO 9001 requires the organization to improve the effectiveness of the quality management system continually through the use of the **quality policy, quality objectives, audit results, analysis of data, corrective** and **preventive actions,** and **management review.**

Application

One can demonstrate the effectiveness of the system simply by producing and examining results against the organization's mission. This does not mean that all the documented policies and procedures are being followed – it means that the system of processes produces results that meet the objectives and that the objectives are relevant to the organization's mission. The processes comprise the activities, resources and behaviours that cause results. The documented policies and procedures are only one part of this; therefore, collecting data on compliance with policies and procedures alone is insufficient to demonstrate effectiveness. Effectiveness is about doing the right things and unless the objectives, policies and procedures are regularly reviewed for relevance, they may be inadvertently driving the organization in the wrong direction.

Ensure

To make certain that something will happen.

Environmental factors of the work environment

Meaning

Environmental factors of the work environment are the factors that impact the product or service being produced or delivered. These are different from the factors that affect the personnel, such as the **physical**, **social** and **psychological** factors.

ISO 9000 requirements and recommendations

Clause 6.4 of ISO 9001 requires the organization to determine and manage the work environment needed to achieve conformity to product requirements. ISO 9000 defines the work environment as a set of conditions under which work is performed and explains that these conditions include physical, social, psychological and environmental factors.

Application

The environmental factors might include:

- Temperature, humidity, light and vibration.
- Particle cleanliness, biological cleanliness and hygiene.
- Magnetic fields, electromagnetic radiation and static electricity.

In dealing with the physical factors there is a series of steps that can be taken to identify and manage these factors:

1 Use scientific research, FMEA or hazards analysis to identify the vulnerability of the product or service to environmental factors.
2 Determine the standard for each factor that needs to be maintained to provide the appropriate environment.
3 Use measurement to discover the prevailing conditions where product is handled or services delivered.
4 Establish whether the standard can be achieved by work space design, by worker control or by management control, or whether protection from the environmental impact is needed.
5 Determine the provisions necessary to eliminate, reduce or control the impact.

6 Put in place the measures that have been determined.
7 Measure and monitor the environment for compliance with the standards and implementation of the provisions defined.
8 Periodically repeat the previous steps to identify any changes that would affect the standards or the provisions currently in place.

Establish and maintain

To set up an entity on a permanent basis, and retain or restore it in a state in which it can fulfil its purpose or required function.

Establishing a management system

Meaning

To 'establish' means to set up on a permanent basis, install or create and, therefore, in establishing a management system, it has to be designed, constructed, resourced, installed and integrated into the organization, signifying that a management system on paper is not a management system. Establishing a system in accordance with the requirements of ISO 9001 means that the characteristics of the system have to meet the requirements of ISO 9001.

The life cycle of the management system has five components:

1 establishing the system;
2 operating the system;
3 evaluating the system;
4 maintaining the system; and
5 improving the system.

ISO 9000 requirements and recommendations

Clause 4.1 of ISO 9001 requires the organization to establish a quality management system in accordance with the requirements of ISO 9001.

Application

Some organizations regard the management system as the way they do things. Merely documenting what you do does not equate with establishing a system that meets the requirements of ISO 9001. Neither does documenting what you do mean that the system will be effective in enabling the organization to achieve its objectives.

There are two primary processes involved in establishing a system once there is agreement on the need: system design and system construction, each of which consists of the following subprocesses.

System design:

● Process identification – determining what processes are required to achieve the organization's objectives.
● Process definition – mapping the processes to a level where tasks and competencies are identified, but methods and procedures are still to be determined.

System construction:

● Process development – determining and defining methods, procedures and techniques, performing prototyping, where necessary, and testing validity.

- Process resourcing – equipping the process with competent people, dependable information and capable equipment.
- Process installation – putting in place the people, methods, controls, linkages, equipment, information, etc.
- Process commissioning – getting everything to work.
- Process integration – stabilizing routines, habits, operating without the help of the process designers.
- Process qualification – testing the capability of the process, verifying conformity and validating performance.
- System integration – validating the linkages between processes and creating seamless operations.
- System qualification – verifying achievement of objectives.

The division between design and construction is not important, but often the detail required for process development is not apparent until parts of the process are working. System design can be performed in isolation of the current management system, but in reality, system construction may not require each subprocess, as many processes may already exist and be adequately defined.

'Installation' is not a term that is often used with respect to a management system. One generally refers to management system 'implementation', but this implies that the management system is a set of rules, not a dynamic system. (You do not implement a product – you implement product design.) As stated previously, in order to establish a management system, one needs to design, resource and install it; therefore, installation is concerned with implementing the design.

Evaluation

Meaning

To ascertain the relative goodness, quality or usefulness of an entity with respect to a specific purpose.

ISO 9000 requirements and recommendations

- Clause 7.3.7 of ISO 9001 requires the review of design and development changes to include evaluation of the effect of the changes on constituent parts and delivered product.
- Clause 7.4.1 of ISO 9001 requires criteria for selection, evaluation and re-evaluation of suppliers to be established and for records of the results of evaluations to be maintained.

Application

Evaluations, whether they are of design changes or of suppliers, need to be performed using agreed criteria. An evaluation without agreed criteria is simply an examination.

In the case of **design changes**, proposals need to be evaluated:

- To validate the reason for change.
- To determine whether the proposed change is feasible.

- To judge whether the change is desirable.
- To determine the effects on performance, costs and timescales.
- To determine the impact of the change on other designs with which it interfaces and in which it is used.
- To examine the documentation affected by the change and, consequently, programme their revision.
- To determine the stage at which the change should be embodied.

In the case of supplier selection, information concerning suppliers needs to be evaluated at several stages in the selection process:

- Preliminary **supplier assessment** performed to select credible suppliers.
- **Pre-qualification of suppliers** performed to select capable bidders.
- Qualification of suppliers performed to qualify capable bidders.
- Tender/quote evaluation performed to select a supplier.

Evidence of conformity

Meaning

Documents which testify that an entity conforms with certain prescribed requirements.

ISO 9000 requirements and recommendations

- Clause 4.2.4 of ISO 9001 requires records to be established and maintained to provide evidence of conformity to requirements and of the effective operation of the quality management system.
- Clause 7.6 of ISO 9001 requires the organization to determine the monitoring and measurement to be undertaken, and the monitoring and measuring devices needed to provide evidence of conformity of product to determined requirements.
- Clause 8.2.4 of ISO 9001 requires evidence of conformity with the acceptance criteria to be maintained.

Application

Evidence of conformity is only valid if produced under controlled conditions – conditions in which the results are the product of planned actions. The evidence should declare the achieved results, the **acceptance criteria** and the authority that makes the declaration. The achieved results should either meet the acceptance criteria or be subject to **concession** approved by the acceptance authority.

Exclusions

Meaning

In the context of ISO 9001, exclusions are the requirements that are deemed outside the scope of the declared quality management system.

ISO 9000 requirements and recommendations

Clause 1.2 of ISO 9001 states that:
  (a) Where any requirement(s) of this International Standard cannot be applied due to the nature of an organization and its product, this can be considered for exclusion.
  (b) Where exclusions are made, claims of conformity to this International Standard are not acceptable unless these exclusions are limited to requirements within clause 7, and such exclusions do not affect the organization's ability, or responsibility, to provide product that fulfils customer and **applicable** regulatory requirements.

Application

The idea that requirements are included or excluded appears to treat the Standard as a design tool, when in fact it is a measurement tool. As a design tool, it suggests that a system is designed to meet the Standard, when in reality, the system is designed to meet business needs. As a measurement tool, if characteristics were missing from the system, they would not be measured and the requirements deemed not applicable. There is a belief that the system is only that which is addressed by the Standard when in reality the system is the means by which the organization's objectives are achieved and, therefore, the question of exclusions does not arise. Exclusion is, therefore, an issue only in connection with certification, not with system design.

If you are seeking certification against ISO 9001, clauses 4, 5 and 8 are mandatory, and any exclusions in clause 7 are only acceptable if they do not affect the organization's ability or responsibility to provide product that meets customer and applicable regulatory requirements. You cannot exclude requirements of clause 7 simply because you do not want to meet them.

The only clause where exclusion is wholly possible is clause 7.5.4 concerning **customer property** because some organizations may not be handed customer property. In all other cases, exclusion is either highly unlikely or partial on the grounds that some requirements of a clause are not applicable.

External documents, control of

Meaning

An external document is one produced externally to the organization's management system.

There are two types of external documents: those in the public domain, and those produced by specific customers and/or suppliers.

ISO 9000 requirements and recommendations

Clause 4.2.4 of ISO 9001 requires the organization to define the controls needed to approve documents for adequacy prior to issue to ensure that documents of external origin are identified and their distribution controlled.

Application

External documents are likely to carry their own identification, which is unique to the issuing authority. If they do not carry a reference number, the issuing authority is normally indicated, which serves to distinguish them from internal documents.

The controls established for external documents should be similar to those established for internal documents, except that the change controls will be different. The organization will be unable to process a change request for public documents and will be limited to transmitting change requests to the issuing authority (such as customers and suppliers) for other external documents. External documents should be reviewed for relevance and approved for use. Mechanisms will be needed to alert users of changes to external documents, and means provided for their withdrawal when obsolete or no longer relevant.

Factual approach

The factual approach is one of the eight quality management principles used as a basis for developing ISO 9000. The principle is expressed as follows. Effective decisions are based on the analysis of data and information. An organization applying the factual approach principle would be one in which people are:

- Taking measurements and collecting data and information relevant to the objective.
- Ensuring the data and information are sufficiently accurate, reliable and accessible.
- Analysing the data and information using valid methods.
- Understanding the value of appropriate statistical techniques.
- Making decisions and taking action based on the results of logical analysis balance with experience and intuition.

Failure mode effects analysis (FMEA)

Meaning

A technique for identifying potential failure modes and assessing existing and planned provisions to detect, contain or eliminate the occurrence of failure. It is essentially a risk assessment technique.

ISO 9000 requirements and recommendations

Clause 8.5.3 of ISO 9004 recommends that, in planning for loss prevention, data can be generated from use of risk analysis tools such as fault mode and effects analysis.

Application

FMEA is a tool that can be used in a variety of situations within an organization. The most common usage is in product and process design as a means of detecting design weaknesses. However, it can equally be used in organization design, management system design or, in fact, any situation where work is performed to achieve a given objective. You can use the FMEA when planning a meeting, a training event, a re-organization or a computer installation. All you need to do is firstly to identify the factors that affect success and ask:

- How might this part or process fail to meet the requirements?
- What could happen that would adversely affect performance?
- What would an interested party consider to be unacceptable?

Then you proceed to analyse the symptoms as follows:

1 Identify the potential effects of failure in terms of what the customer of the output might notice or experience.
2 Determine the severity of the effect. A numerical range of 1–10 can be used to grade severity, with 10 being hazardous without warning and 1 having no effect.
3 Classify the effect in terms of whether it is critical, key, major or significant.
4 Identify the potential cause(s)/mechanism(s) of failure.
5 Determine the occurrence. The likelihood that a specific cause/mechanism will occur – a numerical range of 1–10 can be used for probability of occurrence, with 10 being almost inevitable and 1 being unlikely.
6 Identify current design/process controls in terms of the prevention, verification or other activities to assure process adequacy.
7 Estimate the probability of detection. A numerical range of 1–10 can be used for detection probability, with 10 meaning that the control will not detect the potential failure and 1 meaning that the control will almost certainly detect the potential cause of failure.
8 Calculate the risk priority number. This is the number 1–1000 generated from multiplying the severity, occurrence and detection factors. This element is not essential but does make the result numerical and hence comparable. The higher the result the higher priority needs to be given to it.

First-party audit

Audits of a company or parts thereof by personnel engaged by the company. These audits are also called **internal audits.**

Follow-up audit

Meaning

An audit carried out following and as a direct consequence of a previous audit to determine whether agreed actions have been taken and are effective.

ISO 9000 requirements and recommendations

Clause 8.2.2 of ISO 9001 requires that follow-up activities (audits) include the verification of the actions taken and the reporting of verification results.

Application

- Follow-up action is necessary to verify that the agreed action has been taken and that the original nonconformity has been eliminated.
- Do perform follow-up audits immediately after the planned completion date for the actions or relatively close to the agreed completion date.
- Don't be too concerned that the auditor who carries out the follow-up audit is not the same person who carried out the initial audit. In fact, there is some merit in using different auditors in order to calibrate the auditors.
- Remember the audit remains incomplete until all actions have been verified as being completed.

- Should any action not be carried out by the agreed date, the auditor needs to make a judgement as to whether it is reasonable to set a new date or to escalate the slippage to higher management.
- For minor problems, when there are more urgent priorities facing the managers, setting a new date may be prudent. However, you should not do this more than once.
- Not meeting the agreed completion date is indicative either of a lack of commitment or poor estimation of time. Both indicate that there may well be a more deep-rooted problem to be resolved.

Functions

Meaning

Much confusion exists over the use of the word 'function'. In the organizational sense, a function is a special or major activity (often unique in the organization), which is needed in order for the organization to fulfil its purpose and mission. In this context, an alternative term would be **business process**. The usage of the term 'function' is much older than the term 'business process' and, in some respects, the latter emerged to overcome the misconceptions surrounding the term 'function'. Examples of functions are design, procurement, personnel, manufacture, marketing, maintenance. etc.

A business function is a collection of activities that make a common and unique contribution to the purpose and mission of the business. Contribution rather than skill or discipline determines function. Function, therefore, is not another word for **department**. Functions are divided by contribution. For example, the design function comprises analytical, problem solving, leadership and drawing skills to name but a few. It may also comprise the disciplines of electrical and mechanical engineering and test engineering.

Departments can be grouped by market, product, location or activity. Several departments can, therefore, serve a single function. One department may perform product design with others performing plant design, tooling design, service design, etc.

ISO 9000 requirements and recommendations

- Clause 5.4.1 of ISO 9001 requires top management to ensure that quality objectives, including those needed to meet requirements for product, are established at relevant functions and levels within the organization.
- Clause 7.3.4 of ISO 9001 requires participants in design and development reviews to include representatives of functions concerned with the design and development stage(s) being reviewed.

Application

Structuring an organization on a functional basis is a way of organizing a business. There is no requirement in ISO 9000 for organizations to be structured as a series of functions. A true functional structure would place people according to the function they served not the discipline or skill they have.

Human resources

Human resources are the people that are available to perform specific work and include all types of labour, such as employees, contractors, consultants, agency staff and part-time staff.

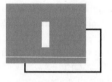

Identification of records

Meaning

Record identification is assigning a characteristic to a record that renders it unique and retrievable.

ISO 9000 requirements and recommendations

Clause 4.2.4 of ISO 9001 requires a documented procedure to be established to define the controls needed for the identification of records.

Application

Records should carry some identification in order that you can determine what they are, what kind of information they record and what they relate to. A simple way of doing this is to give each record a reference number and a name or title in a prominent location on the record.

Where forms are used to collect data, they should carry a form number and name as their identification. When completed they should carry a serial number to give each a separate identity. Records should also be traceable to the product or service they represent, and this can be achieved either within the reference number or separately, provided that the chance of mistaken identity is eliminated.

Identifying document changes

Meaning

It should be possible to establish what has been changed in a document following its revision without laboriously comparing the current and previous versions.

ISO 9000 requirements and recommendations

Clause 4.2.3 of ISO 9001 requires the organization to define the controls needed to ensure that changes to documents are identified.

Application

There are several ways in which you can identify changes to documents:

- By sidelining, underlining, emboldening or similar technique.
- By a change record within the document (front or back) denoting the nature of change.
- By a separate change note that details what has changed and why.
- By appending the change details to the initiating change request.

Identifying processes

Meaning

Process identification has two dimensions:

1 Revealing through examination the inherent processes in an organization that deliver business results.
2 Assigning a characteristic to a process description that renders it unique and retrievable.

ISO 9000 requirements and recommendations

Clause 4.1 of ISO 9001 requires the organization to identify the processes needed for the quality management system.

Application

From the organization's **mission statement** determine the factors upon which accomplishment of the mission depend. These are the critical success factors (CSF). The CSFs indicate the capabilities needed and, consequently, identify the processes required to deliver these capabilities.

In order to fulfil the mission, an organization might need a design capability, a production capability and a distribution capability. This results in a need for a design process, a production process and a distribution process. These processes depend upon an available supply of capital, competent staff, equipment and materials, and well-equipped facilities. Delivery of this capability requires a capable resource management process that manages human, physical and financial resources.

Another CSF would be the ability of the organization to identify customer needs and expectations in its chosen markets and, consequently, a need for an effective marketing process is identified. A further CSF would be the rate at which customer enquiries were converted into sales and, consequently, a need for an effective sales process is identified. By identifying CSFs and the associated processes, a list of core processes will emerge.

The processes identified from the CSFs are the business processes. Each stage of a business process may represent a subprocess and each subprocess may identify work processes and so on until all that is left to identify are the activities required to perform a single task.

Implementation audit

An implementation **audit** is an audit carried out to establish whether work is done in the way it is required to be done, as defined by the documented procedures and instructions. N.B. It is also referred to as a conformance audit or compliance audit.

Infrastructure

Meaning

Infrastructure is the permanent facilities and equipment of an organization. It includes basic facilities, equipment, services and installations needed for functioning and growth of the organization. Such basics would include the buildings and utilities, such as electricity, gas, water and telecommunications. Within the buildings, it would include the office accommodation, furniture, fixtures and fittings, computers, networks, dining areas, medical facilities, laboratories, plant, machinery and, on the site, it would include the access roads and transport. In fact, everything an organization needs to operate other than the financial, human and consumable resources.

ISO 9001 requirement clause 6.3

Clause 6.3 of ISO 9001 requires the organization to determine, provide and maintain the infrastructure needed to achieve conformity to product requirements.

Application

Maintaining the infrastructure implies maintaining the capability the infrastructure provides and, therefore, it is necessary to:

- Identify those assets, including plant, machinery, facilities, networks, etc. upon which the organization depends for its success and which represent its capability.
- Establish a process for reviewing the organization's capability when planning new products, services and processes, and planning the acquisition and deployment of new resources.
- Establish a process that will deliver the new capability in line with the commitments made for the supply of products and services that will use this new capability.
- If there are delays in commissioning new facilities, plant, etc., adjust any corresponding commitments for supply of products and services.
- Establish processes for maintaining buildings, plant and facilities, and making, moving and measuring equipment.
- Establish processes for maintaining services, such as transport, computer networks and telecommunications.
- Make provision for planned and **corrective maintenance**.
- Perform a risk assessment and identify those things on which continuity of business depends – power, water, labour, materials, components, services, etc.
- Determine what could cause a termination of supply and estimate the probability of occurrence.
- Take action to reduce, control or eliminate the probability of failure.
- Prepare contingency plans that will enable the organization to maintain a prescribed level of capability in the event of an emergency, such as utility interruptions, labour shortages, computer failure and equipment breakdown.
- Test the effectiveness of disaster recovery plans periodically.

Inspection

Meaning

The examination of an entity to determine whether it conforms to prescribed requirements.

ISO 9000 requirements and recommendations

- Clause 7.1 of ISO 9001 requires the organization to determine the required inspection activities specific to the product and the criteria for product acceptance.
- Clause 7.4.3 of ISO 9001 requires the organization to establish and implement the inspection activities necessary for ensuring that purchased product meets specified purchase requirements.

Application

In determining inspection activities, you need to determine the probability of an error being detected. If the process is really capable, inspection may not be necessary at all if output can be assured through process controls. If you can be confident that, were you to inspect a characteristic, it would be right, inspection is unnecessary unless regulations apply that require it to be inspected.

Inspection is one means of verification and should be performed as close as possible to the operation that produced the results. The sooner the inspection the sooner any errors are detected. However, inspection can also be left until the stage before the characteristics to be examined are no longer accessible for examination. There is, therefore, a balance to be achieved which should take into account the impact of delaying inspection until the characteristic becomes inaccessible for examination.

Inspection authority

The person or organization that has been given the right to perform inspections. Such personnel may be those producing the product or independent of those producing the product, depending on the risks. Where there is potential for error and the errors are significant to customer satisfaction, independent inspection may be necessary. Error potential can be significantly reduced by employing personnel whose competence is under continual assessment.

Intellectual property

Meaning

Creations of the mind: inventions, literary and artistic works, and symbols, names, images and designs used in commerce. Intellectual property is divided into two categories: industrial property and copyright.

Industrial property is any product of an organization that is original to the organization that created it and may include specifications, designs, processes and techniques, which is why certain organizations are extremely careful about allowing people on to their premises. A competitor that uses the intellectual property of another organization without written permission is in breach of the law.

Copyright property is an original work of an author whereby authors obtain, for a limited time, certain exclusive rights to their works.

ISO 9000 requirements and recommendations

- Clause 6.1.2 of ISO 9004 recommends that consideration should be given to intangible resources to improve the performance of the organization, such as intellectual property.

- Clause 7.5.3 of ISO 9004 suggests that customer property may include intellectual property.

Application

All organizations require knowledge to achieve their objectives. Some knowledge is created within but most comes from outside the organization.

Knowledge and its management is key to survival and external knowledge is a valuable resource that waits to be tapped. The ideas, inventions, designs and other intellectual property that are readily available in the market place should be assessed for their potential to improve the organization's understanding, its management techniques and its products and processes.

When using intellectual property, you have to acknowledge the creator. The Berne Convention of 1988 applies and defines the laws relating to copyright. Copyright protects only an author's original expression. It does not extend to any ideas, system or factual information that is conveyed in a copyrighted work, and it does not extend to any pre-existing material that the author has incorporated into a work.

There is a lot of information on the internet that appears freely available, but you should be careful to check that it is not copyright. Even the graphics may carry a copyright notice. Depending on what you stand to gain by using the intellectual property, you may find yourself or your company being sued for breach of copyright.

Interested party

Meaning

Person or group having an interest in the performance or success of an organization. This includes customers, owners, employees, contractors, suppliers, investors, unions, partners or society.

ISO 9000 requirements and recommendations

- Clause 0.1 of ISO 9004 states that the purpose of an organization is to identify and meet the needs and expectations of its customers and other interested parties.
- Clause 0.2 of ISO 9004 states that the Standard promotes the adoption of a process approach when developing, implementing and improving the effectiveness and efficiency of a quality management system to enhance interested party satisfaction by meeting interested party requirements.

Application

Although ISO 9001 only addresses customers and not the other interested parties, any organization should be clearly focused on satisfying all interested parties if it is to sustain profitability and respect in the community.

The organization's management should, therefore, address all interested parties not simply the needs of customers. While customers may be important, without the support of the other interested parties, the organization is unlikely to survive.

The influence of customers

A product that possesses features that satisfy customer needs is a quality product. Likewise, one that possesses features that dissatisfy customers is not a quality product. So the final arbiter on quality is the customer. The customer acquires a product for the benefits that possession will bring. Therefore, if the product fails to deliver the expected benefits, it will be considered by the customer to be of poor quality.

The influence of suppliers

Suppliers are interested in the success of the organization because it may, in turn, lead to their success. However, suppliers are also stakeholders because they can withdraw their patronage. They can choose their customers. If you treat your suppliers badly, such as delaying payment of invoices, you may find they terminate the supply at the first opportunity, putting your organization at risk relative to its customer commitments.

The influence of investors

Often the most common type of stakeholder (owners, investors including banks and shareholders) are interested in protecting their stake in the business. They will withdraw their stake if the organization fails to perform. Poorly conceived products and poorly managed processes and resources will not yield the expected return, and the action of investors can directly affect the supply chain. Although they are not customers, they are feeding the supply chain with much needed resources.

The influence of employees

Employees may not be interested in the products and services, but are interested in the conditions in which they are required to work. Employees can withdraw their labour and put the organization at risk relative to its commitment to its customers.

Internal audit

Meaning

Internal **audits** are audits of a company or parts thereof by personnel engaged by the company. These audits are also called first-party audits.

An internal audit need not be limited to any aspect of the organization's operations but, when it is, it may be qualified by an adjective such as internal *quality* audits, internal *safety* audits, internal *financial* audits, etc.

ISO 9000 requirements and recommendations

Clause 8.2.2 of ISO 9001 requires internal audits to be conducted at planned intervals to determine whether the quality management system:

- conforms to the planned arrangements;
- conforms to the requirements of ISO 9001;
- conforms to the quality management system requirements established by the organization;
- is effectively implemented and maintained.

Application

Audits performed to determine whether the quality management system conforms to planned arrangements should be designed to verify that the system is capable of:

- implementing the agreed policies (a **policy audit**);
- enabling the organization to achieve the agreed objectives (a **strategic audit**); and
- enabling the organization to meet specific product or project requirements (a **project audit** or **product audit**), and process objectives (a **process audit**).

Audits performed to determine whether the quality management system conforms to ISO 9001 can be conducted in one of two ways:

1 by performing a full internal system audit against ISO 9001; and
2 by analysing the results of policy, strategic, project and process audits, and determining conformity by correlation.

Audits performed to determine whether the quality management system is being effectively implemented and maintained can be conducted in one of three ways:

1 by system implementation audits;
2 by **process audits** conducted by personnel external to the process;
3 by process audits conducted by personnel operating the process.

Internal communication

Meaning

Communication processes are those processes that convey information and impart understanding upwards, downwards and laterally within the organization. They form an essential part of other processes to enable them to function effectively.

ISO 9000 requirements and recommendations

Clause 5.5.3 of ISO 9001 requires top management to ensure that appropriate communication processes are established within the organization and that communication takes place regarding the effectiveness of the quality management system.

Application

Effective communication consists of four steps: attention, understanding, acceptance and action. It is not just the sending of messages from one source to another. Communication has not taken place until action has been accomplished as intended. However, action may be delayed due to the availability of resources or the **motivation** of the personnel involved, which is why it is important to establish that resources and motivation for action (if any) are adequate before initiating communication.

Information needs to be communicated to people for them to perform their role as well as possible. These processes need to be effective otherwise:

- The wrong information will be transmitted.
- The right information will fail to be transmitted.
- The right information will go to the wrong people.
- The right information will reach the right people before they have been prepared for it.
- The right information will reach the right people too late to be effective.

- The communication will not achieve understanding.
- The communication will cause entirely the wrong result.

Within each process take account of:

- The audience as it influences the language, style and approach to be used – 'What are they?'.
- The location as it influences the method – 'Where are they?'.
- Urgency as it influences the method and timing when the information should be transmitted – 'When is it needed?'.
- Sensitivity as it influences the distribution of the information – 'Who needs to know?'.
- Impact as it influences the method of transmission and the competency of the sender – 'How should they be told and who should tell them?'.
- Permanency as it influences the medium used – 'Is it for the moment or the future?'.

To encourage reporting of **system effectiveness**, there needs to be an environment in which staff feel free to report problems, even if their perception of the problems may not be shared by management. An environment in which management filter suggestions in the belief that the suggestions are misguided demonstrates that the communication process is ineffective. Such situations should be used as opportunities for education.

Internal customer

We tend to think of products and services being supplied to customers and also think of internal and external customers but, in reality, there is no such thing as an internal customer. Customers are **stakeholders**; they have entered into a commitment in return for some benefits that possession of a product or experience of a service may bring. The internal receivers of products are stakeholders in the organization, not in the product, and therefore are not customers. ISO 9000:2000 defines the customer as an organization or person that receives a product. It is implied that the organization and person referred to is external to the organization supplying the product. Also the product that is referred to in ISO 9001 is product intended for, or required by, a customer. To interpret the term 'customer' as either internal or external would make nonsense of the requirements in ISO 9001 where the term 'customer' is used. There is no contract between a person who passes output to another person in the same organization. There is or should be a mutually beneficial relationship whereby the receiver should expect any inputs to be complete and correct.

Invitation to tender

Meaning

An invitation to tender (ITT) is an opportunity to offer products and/or services in response to an identified need.

ISO 9000 requirements and recommendations

- Clause 7.2.2 of ISO 9001 requires the organization to review the requirements related to the product prior to the organization's commitment to supply a product to the customer (e.g. submission of tenders, acceptance of contracts or orders, and acceptance of changes to contracts or orders).

- Clause 7.4.2 of ISO 9001 requires the organization to ensure the adequacy of specified purchase requirements prior to their communication to the supplier. (This could include invitations to tender, request for quotation, contracts, subcontracts, etc.)

Application

Organizations issue ITTs to bidders they believe are capable of offering the kind of product or service they require. ITTs are not generally issued to suppliers in the hope that one may come forward with the right capability. The ITT is preceded by a qualification process that selects capable bidders. If you are on the receiving end, they should be treated as required by clause 7.2.2 of ISO 9001. If you are on the issuing end, they should be treated as required by clause 7.4.2 of ISO 9001.

ITTs are normally used to seek a line-by-line response to technical, commercial and managerial requirements. At this stage, you may select a number of potential suppliers and require each to demonstrate its capability. You know what they do but you need to know if they have the capability of producing a product with specific characteristics and can control its quality.

Involvement of people

Involvement of people is one of the eight quality management principles used as a basis for developing ISO 9000. The principle is expressed as follows: 'People at all levels are the essence of an organization and their full involvement enables their abilities to be used for the organization's benefit'.

An organization applying the 'involvement of people' principle would be one in which people are:

- Accepting ownership and responsibility to solve problems.
- Actively seeking opportunities to make improvements.
- Actively seeking opportunities to enhance their competencies, knowledge and experience.
- Freely sharing knowledge and experience in teams and groups.
- Focusing on the creation of value for customers.
- Being innovative and creative in furthering the organization's objectives.
- Better representing the organization to customers, local communities and society at large.
- Deriving satisfaction from their work.
- Enthusiastic and proud to be part of the organization.

ISO 9000

Meaning

ISO 9000 is an international standard that specifies the fundamental concepts and vocabulary associated with quality management systems.

Purpose

The purpose of ISO 9000 is to facilitate common understanding of the concepts and language used in the ISO 9000 family of standards.

Intent

The intent of ISO 9000 is that it be used in conjunction with ISO 9001 and ISO 9004.

Scope

ISO 9000 defines the principles, the fundamental concepts and the terms used in the family of standards. It contains 81 definitions and no requirements.

Applicability

Applies only to the concepts and terms used in the ISO 9000 family of standards. They are not the only concepts and definitions in the field of quality management.

ISO 9000 family

Purpose

The purpose of the ISO 9000 family of international standards is to assist organizations implement and operate effective quality management systems.

Intent

The intent of the ISO 9000 family of international standards is to facilitate mutual understanding in national and international trade, and help organizations achieve sustained success.

Scope

The scope of the ISO 9000 family of international standards is limited to quality management systems.

There are four standards in the family:

- ISO 9000: Quality management systems – Fundamentals and vocabulary.
- ISO 9001: Quality management systems – Requirements.
- ISO 9004: Quality management systems – Guidelines for performance improvements.
- ISO 19011: Guidelines on quality and/or environmental management systems auditing.

Applicability

The ISO 9000 family of standards apply to all organizations regardless of type, size and product provided.

ISO 9001

Purpose

The purpose of ISO 9001 is to provide an equitable basis for assessing the capability of organizations to meet customer and **applicable regulatory requirements**. It is, therefore, a test specification for a quality management system.

Intent

The intent of ISO 9001 is that it can be used for contractual, **certification** or **assessment** purposes. The standard is not intended to be used to design or develop a quality management system.

Scope

ISO 9001 defines the requirements for a quality management system, the purpose of which is to enable organizations to satisfy their customers' needs and expectations continually.

The criteria relate to organizations and not products. There are no product acceptance criteria in ISO 9000. The Standard contains eight sections, 51 clauses and over 250 requirements.

Applicability

ISO 9001 applies where an organization needs to demonstrate its ability to provide product that meets customer and applicable regulatory requirements and aims to enhance **customer satisfaction**. Where the interested parties do not require an organization to demonstrate capability, ISO 9001 does not apply but it can be used as a basis for assessing the capability of an organization. It is not intended to be used as a design specification for a quality management system.

ISO 9004

Purpose

To assist organizations satisfy the needs and expectations of all interested parties.

Intent

It is intended for organizations whose top management wishes to move beyond the requirements of ISO 9001 in pursuit of continual improvement. It is not intended as a guide to meeting the requirements of ISO 9001.

Scope

ISO 9004 provides guidelines for improving the performance of the organization and the satisfaction of all interested parties. It has a similar structure to ISO 9001 to assist in their application as a consistent pair. The Standard contains eight sections and 64 clauses, but no requirements.

Applicability

ISO 9004 applies to organizations seeking guidance on developing quality management systems and improving their performance. It may be used to assist the design and development of a quality management system.

Issue status

The 'issue status' of a document is a term used to describe the maturity of a document. A document may be:

- In draft form, in which case its issue status is *draft*.
- In its approved form, in which case its issue status could be *issue 1, issue 2, issue 3,* etc.
- Withdrawn from use, in which case its issue status is *obsolete*.

N.B. Another term used is **revision status**.

Leadership

Leadership is one of the eight quality management principles used as a basis for developing ISO 9000. The principle is expressed as follows: 'Leaders establish unity of purpose and direction of the organization. They should create and maintain the internal environment in which people can become fully involved in achieving the organization's objectives'.

An organization applying the leadership principle would be one in which leaders are:

- Being proactive and leading by example.
- Understanding and responding to changes in the external environment.
- Considering the needs of all interested parties.
- Establishing a clear **vision** of the organization's future.
- Establishing shared values and ethical role models at all levels of the organization.
- Building trust and eliminating fear.
- Providing people with the required resources and freedom to act with responsibility and accountability.
- Promoting open and honest communication.
- Educating, training and coaching people.
- Setting challenging goals and targets.
- Implementing strategy to achieve these goals and targets.

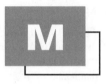

Maintenance

Meaning

Maintenance is the action of retaining something in a serviceable or proper condition. There are several types of maintenance:

- **Corrective maintenance** – maintenance taken in response to a failure.
- **Preventive maintenance** – maintenance taken to prevent failure.
- **Predictive maintenance** – maintenance taken in response to signals from sensors that indicate degradation.
- Planned maintenance – maintenance carried out with forethought as to what is to be checked, adjusted, replaced, etc. Planned maintenance includes preventive and predictive maintenance.

ISO 9000 requirements and recommendations

There are 23 references to maintenance in ISO 9001 – only the principal ones are mentioned here.

- Clause 4.1 of ISO 9001 requires the organization to maintain a quality management system.
- Clause 4.2.4 of ISO 9001 requires records to be maintained to provide evidence of conformity to requirements and of the effective operation of the quality management system.
- Clause 5.4.2 of ISO 9001 requires the integrity of the quality management system to be maintained when changes to the quality management system are planned and implemented.
- Clause 5.5.2 of ISO 9001 requires a member of management to have responsibility and authority for ensuring that processes needed for the quality management system are maintained.
- Clause 6.1 of ISO 9001 requires the organization to determine and provide the resources needed to maintain the quality management system.
- Clause 6.3 of ISO 9001 requires the organization to determine, provide and maintain the infrastructure needed to achieve conformity to product.
- Clause 7.6 of ISO 9001 requires the organization to conduct internal audits to determine whether the quality management system is effectively implemented and maintained.

Application

All but two of the 23 requirements on maintenance address documentation. This illustrates the degree of duplication in ISO 9001 but it should not be assumed that in order to meet other requirements you do not have to maintain things. In the context of the management system, maintenance involves:

- Maintaining knowledge, including intelligence about competitors, markets, technologies, etc.
- Maintaining the capability of processes.
- Maintaining the capability of physical resources, including tools, equipment and infrastructure.
- Maintaining accessibility to material resources.
- Maintaining the availability of financial resources.
- Maintaining the competence of personnel, their skills and knowledge.
- Maintaining information, including the vehicles used for storing it such as paper, film, magnetic disks and tape.

In maintaining processes, you need to keep:

- Reducing variation.
- Physical resources operational.
- Human resources competent.
- Financial resources available for replenishment of consumables, and replacement of worn out or obsolete equipment.
- Process documentation up to date as changes in the organization, technology, resources occur.
- Space available to accommodate input and output.
- Buildings, land and office areas clean and tidy – remove the waste.
- Benchmarking processes against best in the field.

In maintaining capability, you need to keep:

- Replenishing human resources as staff retire, leave the business or are promoted.
- Renewing technologies to retain market position and performance.
- Surplus resources available for unforeseen circumstances.
- Knowledge up to date with the latest industry practices.
- Refreshing **awareness** of the vision, values and mission.

Management commitment

Meaning

In the context of ISO 9000 requirements management **commitment** means:

- A belief that the quality management system is the means by which the organization's objectives are achieved.
- A belief that the reason the organization exists is to create and retain satisfied customers, and that this will only be achieved if everyone in the organization is **customer focused**.
- A belief that the organization has many stakeholders whose requirements need to be met in addition to those of customers.
- A belief that the manner in which the organization pursues its objectives, i.e. its policies, has a direct bearing on its survivability.

- A belief that without measurable objectives and the commensurate resources, goals will remain dreams.
- A belief that continual monitoring and improvement is required to steer the organization towards its goals.

ISO 9000 requirements and recommendations

- Clause 5.1 of ISO 9001 requires top management to provide evidence of its commitment to the development and implementation of the quality management system and continually improving its **effectiveness**.
- Clause 5.3 of ISO 9001 requires top management to ensure that the quality policy includes a commitment to comply with requirements and continually improve the effectiveness of the quality management system.
- In 7.2.2 of ISO 9001 requires the organization to conduct a review of requirements related to the product prior to the organization's commitment to supply a product to the customer.

Application

There is no doubt that actions speak louder than words and it is only when the words are tested that it is revealed whether the writers were serious. It is not about whether management can be trusted but whether they understand the implications of what they have committed themselves to.

The quality policy is the corporate policy of the organization and can, therefore, be considered as the values, beliefs and rules that guide actions, decisions and behaviours.

Commitment begins with a desire to learn, which turns into an awareness once the fundamental principles involved are acknowledged – transmission of information is, therefore, the starting point.

Awareness turns into understanding when those concerned appreciate what they need to do, why they need to do it and what resources they need to do it. A dialogue between transmitter and receiver using the right language coupled with examples, case studies and past experience leads to better understanding. Without the resources to make it happen and knowledge of how they will be deployed and utilized, understanding will not turn into action.

Only when actions are being taken and these actions match the intent is there commitment.

In securing management commitment:

- Do not develop a quality management system simply to obtain certification.
- Drop the word 'quality', if necessary, and call it the business management system.
- Do not refer to the management system as the set of procedures – this is only a partial description of the system.
- Use the system to enable the organization to achieve its objectives.

Management representative

Meaning

The management representative is a person with delegated authority and responsibility to plan, organize and control the quality management system. This manager should act as a co-ordinator, a facilitator, a change agent and should induce change through others.

The appointed person carries the wishes of management (i.e. the policies) to the workforce so that the workforce makes decisions that take into account the wishes (policies) of management.

This person also interfaces with external bodies on matters pertaining to the management system and its capability.

ISO 9000 requirements and recommendations

Clause 5.5.2 of ISO 9001 requires top management to appoint a member of management who ensures that processes needed for the quality management system are established, implemented and maintained, and reports on the need for continual improvement and promotes **awareness** of **customer requirements** throughout the organization.

Application

The objective in this instance is to establish and maintain a coherent and effective management system that enables the organization to achieve its strategic objectives. This will not happen by chance or by collective responsibility – someone has to lead; hence the purpose of this requirement. This role does not usurp that of other managers. Managers produce results using a system that is managed by another manager working cooperatively to achieve a common goal. Someone has to lead the effort required, to direct resources and priorities, and judge the resultant effectiveness.

It is not simply a question of choosing someone to do a job. A number of actions and decisions are needed:

- Define the role of the management representative within the organization.
- Define the competency needed to fulfil the role.
- Select a member of top management who is respected by the other managers and who has the necessary abilities.
- Assign to this person the responsibility for establishing, maintaining and improving the management system.
- Delegate the necessary authority for this person to discharge the responsibilities, i.e. to acquire the necessary resources, evaluate performance and require action to improve system effectiveness.
- Ensure that responsibility for using the system and the outputs from individual processes remains with the other managers.
- Evaluate and develop his/her competency to perform the role effectively.
- Ensure each process has provision for data collection on process performance that can be accessed by the management representative.

Management review

Meaning

The management **review** is top management looking again at the quality management system to establish how well it enables the organization to fulfil its objectives.

It is not a meeting but a review of information on the organization's performance by those responsible for that performance. A meeting might be necessary simply to agree actions.

ISO 9000 requirements and recommendations

- Clause 5.1 of ISO 9001 requires top management to improve the **effectiveness of the quality management system** continually by conducting management reviews.
- Clause 5.6.1 of ISO 9001 requires top management to review the organization's quality management system, at planned intervals, to ensure its continuing suitability, adequacy and effectiveness. (This is duplicated in clause 8.5.1.)
- Clause 5.6.2 of ISO 9001 requires inputs to management review to include information on audits, customer feedback, process performance and product conformity, the status of preventive and corrective actions, follow-up actions from previous management reviews, changes that could affect the quality management system, and recommendations for improvement.
- Clause 5.6.3 of ISO 9001 requires outputs from the management review to include any decisions and actions related to resource needs, and improvement of the effectiveness of the quality management system and its products and processes.

Application

The management review is simply part of the **business management process**. It does not need to be a single review. Management reviews can be carried out on each process as part of the management of that process. Management reviews can be carried out on each division, on each site of an organization. The notion that it has to be only a high level event is unfounded. How many reviews are needed to assess the suitability, adequacy and effectiveness of the management system is a matter for the organization to consider.

Suitability in this context means establishing that the results are being achieved in the best way. If the quality management system is inefficient, the organization may not be able to continue to feed a resource hungry system.

Adequacy in this context means establishing that the outputs meet requirements. If the system delivers product or service that fails to meet customer requirements, then it can hardly be considered adequate.

Effectiveness in this context means establishing that the system fulfils its purpose. The system may deliver satisfied customers and minimize use of resources but, if it is not responding to the changing needs of society, of customers, of regulators and of other interested parties, it is not an effective system.

There are a number to actions that are necessary before, during and after the review.

Before:

- Identify the organization's objectives at strategic, process and product levels.
- Determine how performance will be measured against each objective.

During:

- Collect the data.
- Analyse the data.
- Review the data and identifying opportunities for improvement.
- Meet with senior managers to discuss and agree the results.
- Decide the course of action to improve performance.

After:

- Define new performance baselines.
- Notify staff of the results of the review.

- Execute the agreed actions before the date required.
- Track progress of actions and update the action log.

Marketing process

Meaning

The marketing process is one of the core **business processes**. It delivers new opportunities into the order fulfilment process, so that new or modified products or services can be created to satisfy market needs. The process also predicts customer future needs, which are fed into the business management process, where the organizational strategy is formed and deployed.

ISO 9000 requirements and recommendations

There are no specific requirements in ISO 9001 for a marketing process. However, there are requirements for the determination of customer needs and expectations as well as regulatory requirements, for **awareness** of customer requirements. ISO 9004 recommends competitor analysis, benchmarking and other marketing techniques. The **customer focus** principle emphasizes the importance of understanding both current and future **customer needs**.

Application

Whether or not you have a marketing department, you have a marketing process. No organization can survive without understanding the needs and expectation of its customers – and this is what marketing is all about. In some organizations, the term 'marketing' relates to selling but this is a separate process with different objectives. The objectives of the marketing process are to understand the environment in which the organization operates and identify opportunities for fulfilling unsatisfied needs. This will result in requirements for new products and services, abandoning existing products and services, seeking new markets, withdrawing from exhausted markets. A model marketing process is illustrated in the figure.

Measurement

Measurement is the assignment of numbers to the characteristics of an entity.

Measurement capability

Measurement capability is the ability of a measuring system to measure true values to the accuracy and precision required.

Measurement process

A measurement process consists of the measurement objective (what is to be measured), operations (the measurement tasks and the environment in which they are carried out), the procedures (how the measurement tasks are performed), devices (gauges, instruments, software, techniques, etc. used to make the measurements) and the personnel designated to assign a quantity to the characteristics being measured.

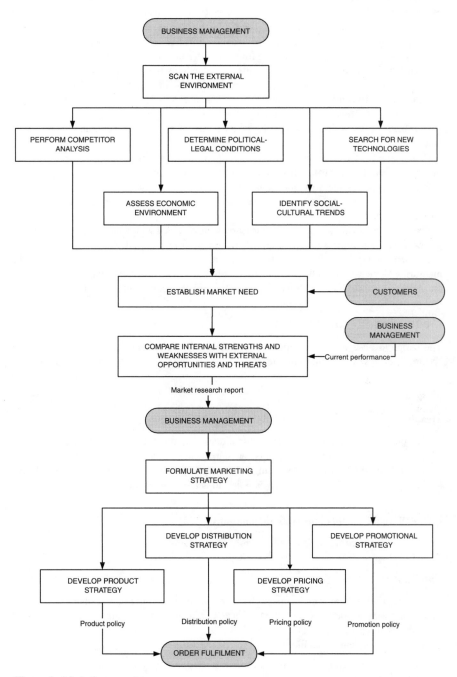

Figure 6   Marketing process

This is also referred to as a measurement system, which is not the same as a system of measurement. A system of measurement refers to the conventions used for the units of measurement, e.g. metric system, CGS system or Imperial system.

In a measurement system, the physical signal is compared with a reference signal of known quantity. The reference signal is derived from measures of known quantity by a process called **calibration**. The known quantities are based on standards that in the majority of cases are agreed internationally. Measurement processes must be in **statistical control** so that all variation is due to common cause and not special cause. Variation in measurement processes arises due to bias, repeatability, reproducibility, stability and linearity.

Bias is the difference between the observed average of the measurements and the reference value.

Repeatability is the variation in measurements obtained by one appraiser using one measuring device to measure an identical characteristic on the same part.

Reproducibility is the variation in the average of the measurements made by different appraisers using the same measuring instrument when measuring an identical characteristic on the same part.

Stability is the total variation in the measurements obtained with a measurement system on the same part when measuring a single characteristic over a period of time.

Linearity is the difference in the bias values through the expected operating range of the measuring device. It is only possible to supply parts with identical characteristics if the measurement processes as well as the production processes are under statistical control.

Measurement uncertainty

The variation observed when repeated measurements of the same parameter on the same specimen are taken with the same device.

Mission

Meaning

In the context of management, a mission is a quest, a journey to a destination in which the whole organization is engaged. The mission statement tells us what our goal is – where are we going. It provides the compass setting for the organization. It is the foundation of effective leadership. It is how the organization is going to achieve its **vision**.

ISO 9000 requirements and recommendations

The term is not used in the ISO 9000 family of standards.

Application

Without customers there is no business, therefore, the basic purpose of a business is to satisfy a particular want in society and so create a customer. Its mission is related to these wants and is expressed in specific terms.

The mission statement should:

- Give clear and unambiguous direction to all who serve the organization.
- Relate to the organizations current and future customers/markets.
- Express the benefits the organization's products or services are to bring to the targeted customer/markets.

- Always look outside the business not inside. For example a mission that is focused on increasing market share is an inwardly seeking mission whereas a mission that is focused on bringing cheap digital communication to the community is an outwardly seeking mission statement.
- Express a shared belief. There is no point in publishing a mission statement when people have not been involved in its development.
- Remain constant despite changes in top management. Too many changes to the mission cause people to pull in different directions.
- Take into account all stakeholders.
- Take the medium-term view (objectives take the short-term view and vision the long-term view).

Only a clear definition of the business purpose and mission makes possible clear and realistic business objectives. It is the starting point for strategies, structures and processes. Processes will not cause the right results unless the process objectives have been derived from the mission.

Modifications

Entities altered or reworked to incorporate design changes.

Monitoring

Meaning

Monitoring means checking periodically and systematically. It does not imply that action will be taken. It is looking for unusual occurrences or indicators of a potential change in performance so that action can be taken to prevent nonconformity.

It differs from measurement in that measurement implies that standards have been set and performance against those standards is being verified.

ISO 9000 requirements and recommendations

- Clause 4.1 of ISO 9001 requires the organization to ensure the availability of resources and information necessary to support the operation and monitoring of the quality management system processes.
- Clause 4.1 of ISO 9001 requires the organization to ensure monitor, measure and analyse the quality management system processes.
- Clause 7.1 of ISO 9001 requires the organization to determine the required verification, validation, monitoring, inspection and test activities specific to the product.
- Clause 7.5.1 of ISO 9001 requires **controlled conditions** to include the availability and use of monitoring and measuring devices, and the implementation of monitoring and measurement.
- Clause 7.5.3 of ISO 9001 requires the organization to identify the product status with respect to monitoring and measurement requirements.
- Clause 7.6 of ISO 9001 requires the organization to determine the monitoring and measurement to be undertaken to provide evidence of conformity of product to determined requirements.

- Clause 7.6 of ISO 9001 requires the organization to establish processes to ensure that monitoring and measurement can be carried out and are carried out in a manner that is consistent with the monitoring and measurement requirements.
- Clause 8.1 of ISO 9001 requires the organization to plan and implement the monitoring, measurement, analysis and improvement processes needed.
- Clause 8.1 of ISO 9001 requires the organization to monitor information relating to customer perception as to whether the organization has fulfilled customer requirements.
- Clause 8.2.3 of ISO 9001 requires the organization to apply suitable methods for monitoring of the quality management system processes.
- Clause 8.2.3 of ISO 9001 requires the organization to monitor and measure the characteristics of the product to verify that product requirements are fulfilled.
- Clause 8.4 of ISO 9001 requires the organization to determine, collect and analyse appropriate data, including data generated as a result of monitoring and measurement.

Application

For process monitoring to be effective, the staff involved need to understand the process objectives and how they are measured. They need to be vigilant to potential and actual variations from the norm.

When designing the process for producing product or delivering service, you should have provided stages at which product/service features are verified and/or installed monitoring devices that indicate when the standard operating conditions have been achieved and whether they are being maintained.

The monitoring devices need to be accessible to process operators for information on the performance of the process to be obtained. The monitoring devices may be located in inaccessible places providing the signals are transmitted to the operators controlling the process.

Monitoring and measuring devices

Meaning

Monitoring and measurement devices are gauges, instruments, sensors, tools and techniques used for monitoring and measuring characteristics.

Mechanical and electronic equipment are the most common monitoring and measurement devices. However, sensors, surveys and assessment of customer satisfaction, competition, supplier performance, personnel competency are also monitoring and measuring devices.

ISO 9000 requirements and recommendations

Clause 7.6 of ISO 9001 requires the organization to determine the monitoring and measuring devices needed to provide evidence of conformity of product to determined requirements.

Application

When identifying measuring and monitoring devices, you need to identify the characteristic, the unit of measure and the target value, and then choose an appropriate measuring or monitoring device. It is relatively easy to identify measuring and monitoring devices for hardware product and processes material, but less easy for services, software and information.

When designing a process for producing product or delivering service, you should have provided stages at which product/service features are verified and/or installed monitoring devices that indicate when the standard operating conditions have been achieved and whether they are being maintained. The devices used to perform measurements need to be available where the measurements are to be performed. The monitoring devices need to be accessible to process operators without abnormal movement for information on the performance of the process to be obtained. The monitoring devices may be located in inaccessible places providing the signals are transmitted to the operators controlling the process.

It is not necessary to calibrate all monitoring devices. Some devices may be used solely as an indicator, such as a thermometer, a clock or a tachometer – other equipment may be used for diagnostic purposes, to indicate if a fault exists. If such devices are not used for determining the acceptability of products and services or **process parameters**, their calibration is not essential.

Motivation

Motivation is an inner mental state that prompts a direction, intensity and persistence in behaviour.

Everything achieved in or by an organization ultimately depends upon the activities of its workforce. It is, therefore, imperative that the organization is staffed by people who are motivated to achieve its goals. All personnel are motivated but not all are motivated to achieve their organization's goals. Many may be more interested in achieving their personal goals.

Motivation is key to performance. The performance of a task is almost always a function of three factors: environment, ability and motivation. To maximize performance of a task, personnel have not only to have the necessary ability or competence to perform it, but also need to be in the right surroundings and have the motivation to perform it.

Mutual beneficial supplier relationships

Mutual beneficial supplier relationships is one of the eight quality management principles used as a basis for developing ISO 9000. The principle is expressed as follows: 'An organization and its suppliers are interdependent and a mutually beneficial relationship enhances the ability of both to create value'.

An organization applying the supplier relationship principle would be one in which people are:

- Identifying and selecting key suppliers.
- Establishing supplier relationships that balance short-term gains with long-term considerations for the organization and society at large.
- Creating clear and open **communications with customers** and suppliers.
- Initiating joint development and improvement of products and processes.
- Jointly establishing a clear understanding of customers' needs.
- Sharing information and future plans.
- Recognizing supplier improvements and achievements.

The principle applies to the organization both as a customer and as a supplier.

Naming processes

There are two conventions used for naming processes: one is verb-focused and the other is noun-focused. The verb-focused construction of a process name commences with a verb, such as produce, define or acquire. The noun-focused construction may simply be one word, such as marketing, design or production.

The noun-focused convention can give the impression that the chain of processes is a chain of departmental functions having these titles, when in reality several departmental functions might contribute to each process. In order to avoid the confusion, it may be more appropriate to use the verb-focused convention or choose names that are different from the **functions** or **departments**.

In order to avoid using departmental names, organizations are being more descriptive in the naming of processes and identifying the purpose of the process within its name, such as the *order to cash process* or the *understanding customer needs process*.

Nonconforming product

Meaning

Nonconforming product is product or service that does not conform to specified requirements for the product or service under examination.

A product that does not conform to requirements specified for a product different to the one being examined is not nonconforming – it is simply different.

ISO 9000 requirements and recommendations

Clause 8.3 of ISO 9001 requires the organization to ensure that product which does not conform to product requirements is identified and controlled to prevent its unintended use or delivery.

Application

In order to control a nonconforming product or service, there are a number of actions you need to take before, during and after the nonconformity is detected.

Before:

1 Decide on who the acceptance authority is to be for each product, project or contract for each class of nonconformity.

2 Develop a means of classifying nonconformities.
3 Prepare procedures, labels and forms for processing nonconforming articles and controlling quarantine areas.

During:

1 Identify the product that is suspected of being nonconforming.
2 Confirm the nonconformity.
3 Check other articles if the nonconformity appears to be symptomatic of the producing process.
4 Record the nature of the nonconformity in terms of the required and actual condition.
5 Segregate the nonconforming product from conforming products.
6 Submit the nonconformity record to the acceptance authority for a decision.
7 Confirm that any previous remedial actions for this type of nonconformity were successful.
8 Consider the cost of replacement against the cost of rework or repair.
9 Do not change the design by means of a nonconformity report or concession.
10 Record the decision of the acceptance authority.
11 Take the action that has been authorized.
12 Verify reworked or repaired product against the original specification.
13 Record the results of the verification.
14 Release conforming product or dispose of product that cannot be re-graded or re-used.

After:

1 Keep the records of the nature of nonconformity, the disposition and the result of post-remedial action verification together.
2 Analyse nonconformity data for trends and conditions that indicate that the process is out of control.

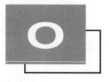

Objective

An objective is a result that is to be achieved usually by a given time. It is what you are trying to do or what the organization is trying to do, or what the process is intended to accomplish.

SMART is a technique to test the robustness of objectives, meaning that objectives should be specific, measurable, achievable, realistic and timely.

Specific: Objectives should be specific actions completed in executing a strategy. They should be derived from the **mission** and relevant to the process or task to which they are being applied. They should be specified to a level of detail that those involved in their implementation fully understand what is required for their completion.

Measurable: Objectives should be measurable actions having a specific end condition. They should be expressed in terms that can be measured using available technology. When setting objectives, you need to know how achievement will be indicated, and the conditions or performance levels that will indicate success.

Achievable: Objectives should be achievable with resources that can be made available and achievable by average people applying average effort.

Realistic: Objectives should be realistic in the context of the current climate, and the current and projected workload. Account needs to be taken of the demands from elsewhere that could jeopardize achievement of the objective.

Timely: Objectives should be time-phased actions that have a specific start and completion date. Time-phased objectives facilitate periodic review of progress and tracking of revisions. (See also **quality objectives**.)

Objective evidence

Objective evidence is information that can be proven true, based on facts obtained through observation, measurement, test or other means.

Obsolete documents

An obsolete document is one that is no longer required for operational purposes.

Order fulfilment process

Meaning

The order fulfilment process converts customer enquiries into satisfied customers. It is one of the core **business processes** of any organization and consolidates the sales, **product realization** and product distribution processes.

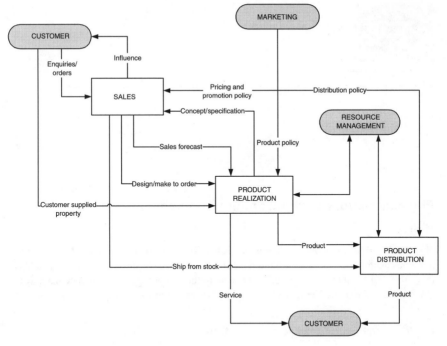

Figure 7   Order fulfilment process

ISO 9000 requirements and recommendations

There are no specific requirements in ISO 9001 or recommendations in ISO 9004 for an order fulfilment process. However, there are requirements for handling enquiries and orders and for product realization including delivery and, therefore, all the constituents of order fulfilment are addressed.

Application

Order fulfilment is a convenient label for all the processes that generate a product or deliver a service. In a pure manufacturing environment, it might be termed *production*, but this term is often the name of a department and, therefore, the term *order fulfilment* enables us to avoid misunderstanding. The label is convenient also because there is an external stakeholder at each end for which objectives can be defined. A typical order fulfilment process is illustrated in the figure.

Organizational goals

Organizational goals are where the organization desires to be, in markets, in innovation, in social and environmental matters, in competition and in financial health.

Physical factors of the work environment

Meaning

Physical factors of the **work environment** include space, temperature, noise, light, humidity, hazards, cleanliness, vibration, pollution, accessibility, physical stress and airflow. In addition to visible light, other types of radiation across the whole spectrum impact the physical environment. These are the factors that affect the people in the workplace.

ISO 9000 requirements and recommendations

Clause 6.4 of ISO 9001 requires the organization to determine and manage the work environment needed to achieve conformity to product requirements. ISO 9000 defines the work environment as a set of conditions under which work is performed and explains that these conditions include physical, **social, psychological** and **environmental** factors.

Application

To manage the physical factors they firstly need to be identified and this requires a study of the work environment to be made relative to its influence on the worker. We are not necessarily dealing only with safety issues, although these are very important. The noise levels do not need to cause harm for them to be a factor that adversely affects worker performance. Libraries are places of silence simply to provide the best environment in which people can concentrate on reading. No harm arises if the silence is broken!

In dealing with physical factors, there is a series of steps you can take to identify and manage these factors:

1 Use an intuitive method, such as brainstorming, to discover the safety-related and non-safety-related factors of the environment.
2 Research legislation and associated guidance literature to identify those factors that could exist in the work environment due to the operation of certain processes, use of certain products or equipment.
3 Determine the standard for each factor that needs to be maintained to provide the appropriate environment.
4 Establish whether the standard can be achieved by work space design, by worker control or management control, or whether protection from the environmental impact is needed.
5 Establish what could fail that would breach the agreed standard using **FMEA** or hazards analysis, and identify the cause and the effect on worker performance.

6 Determine the provisions necessary to eliminate, reduce or control the impact.
7 Put in place the measures that have been determined.
8 Measure and monitor the working environment for compliance with the standards and implementation of the provisions defined.
9 Periodically repeat the previous steps to identify any changes that would affect the standards or the provisions currently in place.

Plan

A plan is the provision made to achieve an objective.

Planned arrangements

Meaning

Planned arrangements are all the arrangements made by the organization to achieve the requirements of the interested parties. They include agreements, **contracts**, proposals, **tenders**, specifications policies, strategies, objectives, plans and processes, and the prescriptive and descriptive documents derived from them.

ISO 9000 requirements and recommendations

- Clause 7.3.4 of ISO 9001 requires systematic reviews of design and development to be conducted in accordance with planned arrangements at suitable stages.
- Clause 7.3.4 of ISO 9001 requires design and development verification to be performed in accordance with planned arrangements.
- Clause 7.3.5 of ISO 9001 requires design and development validation to be performed in accordance with planned arrangements.
- Clause 8.2.2 of ISO 9001 requires the organization to conduct internal audits at planned intervals to determine whether the quality management system conforms to the planned arrangements.
- Clause 8.2.2 of ISO 9001 requires the organization to monitor and measure the characteristics of the product at appropriate stages of the **product realization** process in accordance with the planned arrangements.

Application

This means that, whatever arrangements have been made for conducting design reviews, design verification, audits and monitoring and measuring product, these activities should be carried out as intended.

Policy

A policy is a guide to thinking, action and decision. A policy can, therefore, be anything that constrains actions and decisions.

Policies are essential in ensuring the effective planning of processes because they lay down the rules to be followed to ensure that actions and decisions taken in the design and operation of processes serve the business objectives.

There are different types of policy as listed below.

- Government policy, which when translated into statutes applies to any commercial enterprise.
- Corporate policy, which applies to the business as a whole, and may cover, for example:
  (a) Environmental policy – our intentions with respect to the conservation of the natural environment.
  (b) Financial policy – how the business is to be financed.
  (c) Marketing policy – to what markets the business is to supply its products.
  (d) Investment policy – how the organization will secure the future.
  (e) Expansion policy – the way in which the organization will grow, both nationally and internationally.
  (f) Personnel policy – how the organization will treat its employees and the labour unions.
  (g) Safety policy – the organization's intentions with respect to hazards in the workplace and to users of its products or services.
  (h) Social policy – how the organization will interface with society.
- Operational policy, which applies to the operations of the business, such as design, procurement, manufacture and servicing. This may cover, for example:
  (a) Pricing policy – how the pricing of products is to be determined.
  (b) Procurement policy – how the organization will obtain the components and services needed.
  (c) Product policy – what range of products the business is to produce.
  (d) Inventory policy – how the organization will maintain economic order quantities to meet its production schedules.
  (e) Production policy – how the organization will determine what it makes or buys, and how the production resources are to be organized.
  (f) Servicing policy – how the organization will service the products its customers have purchased.
- Department policy, which applies solely to one department, such as the particular rules a department manager may impose to allocate work, review output, monitor progress, etc.
- Industry policy, which applies to a particular industry, such as the **codes of practice** set by trade associations for a certain trade.

Policy audit

Meaning

A policy **audit** is an examination of written and practised policies to determine the extent to which they align with the mission of the organization.

ISO 9000 requirements and recommendations

There is no specific requirement for a policy audit in ISO 9001 but there is a requirement for audits to determine whether the quality management system conforms to planned arrangements. The mission and objectives of an organization are **planned arrangements**. The guiding principles that condition the actions and decisions people take to accomplish the mission and achieve the objectives are *policies* that are part of the quality management system and, therefore, should be audited.

Application

The policy audit should establish that:

- The corporate policies are derived from an analysis of the factors critical to accomplishment of the organization's purpose – 'Are they soundly based?'.
- The corporate policies are communicated throughout the organization – 'Does everyone understand them?'.
- Measures have been established for determining whether the corporate policies are being implemented – 'How will we know if they are not being implemented?'.
- The operational policies do not conflict with the corporate policies – 'How do departmental policies relate to corporate policies?'.

Potential nonconformity

Meaning

A potential nonconformity is a situation that, if left alone, will in time result in nonconformity.

ISO 9000 requirements and recommendations

Clause 8.3 of ISO 9001 requires the organization to determine action to eliminate the causes of potential nonconformities in order to prevent their occurrence.

Application

See **preventive action**.

Predictive maintenance

Predictive **maintenance** is work scheduled to monitor machine condition, predict pending failure and make repairs on an as-needed basis as part of preventive maintenance. In order to determine the frequency of checks, you need to predict when failure may occur.

In order to determine the frequency of checks, you need to predict when failure may occur. Will failure occur at some future time, after a certain number of operating hours, when being operated under certain conditions or some other time?

An example of predictive maintenance is vibration analysis. Sensors can be installed to monitor vibration and thus give a signal when normal vibration levels have been exceeded. This can signal tool wear and tear in other parts of the machine in advance of the stage where nonconforming product will be generated.

Pre-qualification of suppliers

Pre-qualification of suppliers is the action taken to select suppliers for known future work. It is undertaken to select those suppliers that can demonstrate they have the capability to meet your specific requirements on quality, quantity, price and delivery. A supplier may have the capability to meet quality, quantity and price requirements, but not have the capacity available when you need the product or service. One that has the capacity may not offer the best price and one that meets the other criteria may not be able to supply product in the quantity you require.

Once the list is generated, a request for quotation (RFQ) or invitation to **tender (ITT)** can be issued depending on what is required. RFQs are normally used where price only is required. This enables you to disqualify bidders offering a price well outside your budget. ITTs are normally used to seek a line-by-line response to technical, commercial and managerial requirements. At this stage, you may select a number of potential suppliers and require each to demonstrate its capability. You know what they do but you need to know if they have the capability of producing a product with specific characteristics and can control its quality.

Preservation of product

Meaning

Preservation of product means the action of preventing product from deterioration, damage, degradation, loss of identity, loss of accuracy and loss of integrity.

ISO 9000 requirements and recommendations

Clause 7.5.5 of ISO 9001 requires the organization to preserve the conformity of product during internal processing and delivery to the intended destination, including identification, handling, packaging, storage and protection.

Application

In order to preserve product following processing operations, it is necessary to take several actions before, during and after processing:

- Determine preservation requirements during the design phase or the manufacturing or service planning phase by assessing the risks to product quality during its manufacture, storage, movement, transportation and installation.
- Control packaging design as you would product design.
- Design preservation processes to prolong the life of the product by inhibiting the effect of natural elements.
- Use FMEA or hazard analysis to identify risks.
- Where risks are identified, prepare instructions for the handling, storage, packing, preservation and delivery of particular items.
- Reference instructions in the appropriate work instructions in order that they are implemented when necessary.
- Provide **traceability** from the identification of need to implementation of the provisions and from there to the records of achievement.
- Identify packaging so that it complies with the requirements of home and overseas markets.
- Apply markings to both primary and secondary packaging as well as to the product itself.
- Mark packaging using materials that will survive the conditions of storage and transportation.
- Use marking materials that are resistant to cleaning processes both in the factory and in use.
- Apply markings on packaging to warn handlers of any dangers or precautions they must observe.

- Identify limited-life items so as to indicate their shelf life, ensuring that the expiry date is visible on the container.
- Make provision for limited-life items to be removed from stock when their indicated life has expired.
- For products that start to deteriorate when the packaging seal is broken, apply markings to the containers to warn consumers of the risks.

Prevent

To prevent is to stop something from occurring by a deliberately planned action.

Preventive action

Meaning

Preventive action is action proposed or taken to stop something from occurring. When actual problems do not exist but there is a possibility of failure, however unlikely, the action of preventing the occurrence of this failure (or any problem for that matter) is a preventive action.

ISO 9000 requirements and recommendations

- Clause 5.6.2 of ISO 9001 requires the input to management review to include information on status of preventive actions.
- Clause 8.4 of ISO 9001 requires the analysis of data to provide information relating to opportunities for preventive action.
- Clause 8.5.1 of ISO 9001 requires the organization to improve the **effectiveness of the quality management system** continually through the use of preventive actions.
- Clause 8.5.3 of ISO 9001 requires preventive actions to be appropriate to the effects of the potential problems.
- Clause 8.5.3 of ISO 9001 requires the organization to establish, implement and maintain documented procedures for preventive actions.

Application

The most cost-effective action one can take in any organization is an action designed to prevent problems from occurring. Preventive action, therefore, saves money even though there is a price to pay for the discovery of potential nonconformities.

The action necessary to eliminate, reduce or control the effects of a potential nonconformity may be as simple as applying existing techniques or methods to a new product or process. In other cases it might involve designing new techniques and methods – something that may require additional resources and a development team.

Steps in the preventive action process are as follows:

1 Determine the objectives of the product, process, task or activity.
2 Organize a diagnostic team.
3 Perform an analysis to determine the factors critical to the achievement of these objectives.
4 Determine how the factors might act to affect the product, process, task or activity adversely (the mode of failure).

5 Determine the potential effect of such condition on the achievement of the objectives.

6 Record the criteria for determining severity or priority.

7 Determine the severity of the effect on meeting the objective.

8 Assess the probability of this condition occurring.

9 Postulate causes and test theories.

10 Determine the root cause of potential nonconformity.

11 Identify the provisions currently in place that will prevent this adverse condition occurring or detect it before it has a detrimental effect on performance.

12 Assess the probability that these provisions will prevent this condition occurring or detect it before it has a detrimental effect on performance.

13 Determine any additional action needed to prevent the potential nonconformity occurring.

14 Organize an implementation team.

15 Create or choose the conditions which will ensure effective implementation.

16 Implement the agreed action.

17 Determine whether the actions were those that were required to be taken.

18 Determine whether the actions were performed in the best possible way.

19 Determine whether the nonconformity has occurred.

20 If nonconformity has occurred, undertake corrective action and review the preventive action methods.

It is necessary when considering the requirements for preventive action to avoid limiting your imagination to products. There is likely to be a greater potential for failure in the organization and its processes as in its products.

Preventive maintenance

Preventive **maintenance** is maintenance carried out at predetermined intervals to reduce the probability of failure or performance degradation, e.g. replacing oil filters at defined intervals.

An effective maintenance system should be one that achieves its objectives in minimizing *down time*, i.e. the period of time in which the equipment is not in a condition to perform its function.

Procedure

A procedure is a sequence of steps to execute a routine activity. Procedures do not have to be documented to be considered procedures (see also **documented procedures**).

In contrast, a procedure executes a task or activity, whereas a process achieves an objective.

ISO 9000 defines a procedure as a specified way to carry out an activity or a process. The ambiguity in this definition is that it implies that processes are implemented through procedures. This is not correct. A process is activated by competent people and/or machines executing specific activities with adequate resources to produce required outputs. The order in which the activities are carried out to produce the output may be defined by a procedure.

The characteristics of a procedure are as follows:

- A defined purpose.
- A defined scope and applicability.

- A statement of **responsibilities**.
- Reference documents containing information to be used.
- Instructions as a sequence of tasks to be performed and decisions to be made.
- Documents generated as a result of performing the tasks.

Process

Meaning

A process in its simplest form converts inputs into outputs. The conversion is caused by a series of interrelated tasks, behaviours and resources acting on the inputs. Every result is achieved by a process but it does not mean that the result is one that is required: pollution is caused by a process; nonconforming product is caused by a process. An effective process is one that achieves the results that are intended, i.e. the objectives.

Flow charts may describe the process flow but they are not in themselves processes because they simply define transactions. A series of transactions can represent a chain from input to output but it does not cause things to happen. Add the resources, the behaviours, the constraints and make the necessary connections, and you might have a process that will cause things to happen. Managed processes are processes that cause the right things to happen.

The characteristics of a process are as follows:

- A defined purpose – a reason for existence.
- A defined objective – what results it aims to achieve.
- Inputs in the form of product, people, information, equipment, materials and money.
- Constraints in the form of rules, regulations, laws and policies.
- Resources in the form of tools, equipment, plant, machinery, money, people and knowledge.
- Activities in a sequence from start to finish or entry to exit.
- Controls in the form of standards, measurements and feedback loops.
- Interfaces with other processes feeding inputs or taking outputs.
- Outputs in the form of product, information, people and decisions.
- Outcomes in the form of effects on people, environment, business performance, society and investors.
- Results as a measure of adequacy of outputs.
- Results as a measure of efficiency and effectiveness.

Process approach

The process approach is one of the eight quality management principles used as a basis for developing ISO 9000. The principle is expressed as follows: 'A desired result is achieved more efficiently when activities and related resources are managed as a process'.

An organization applying the process approach principle would be one in which people are:

- Defining the objectives of the organization's processes.
- Defining a process that will achieve specific objectives.
- Establishing clear responsibility, authority and accountability for managing the process.
- Determining the stages in the process necessary to achieve the results.
- Determining the activities required to accomplish each process stage.
- Determining the competence required of the people performing these activities.

- Identifying the inputs and outputs of the process.
- Determining the measurements required to verify process inputs and outputs meet requirements.
- Determining the information and resource requirements needed to achieve the process objectives.
- Determining the sequence and interaction of activities within the process.
- Taking action to prevent use or delivery of nonconforming inputs or outputs until remedial action has been effected.
- Taking action to eliminate the cause of nonconforming inputs or outputs.
- Evaluating possible risks, consequences and impacts of processes on customers, suppliers and other stakeholders of the process.
- Identifying the interfaces between the processes within the organization.
- Identifying the customers, suppliers and other stakeholders of the process.
- Determining the measurements required to establish process efficiency and effectiveness.
- Measuring process outputs, efficiency and effectiveness.
- Aware of the results the process is achieving.

Process audit

Meaning

A process **audit** is an examination of process plans, controls and operations to determine the extent to which the process is capable of achieving the process objectives efficiently and effectively.

ISO 9000 requirements and recommendations

There is no specific requirement for a process audit in ISO 9001 but there is a requirement for audits to determine whether the quality management system (QMS) conforms to the planned arrangements. The objectives for a particular process are **planned arrangements** and, hence, the plans made for achieving process objectives are part of the QMS and, therefore, should be audited. There is also a requirement for audits to determine whether the QMS is being effectively implemented and maintained. As the QMS comprises the organization's processes, audits of the extent to which processes achieve their objectives should, therefore, be performed.

Application

The process audit should not simply examine conformity with prescribed requirements, such as specifications, plans and procedures. It should examine process effectiveness and answer the questions:

- Is the process achieving its objectives?
- Are the objectives being achieved in the best way?
- Are the objectives relevant to the organization's objectives?

In answering the first question, the auditor should establish what the process objectives are and what measures have been defined for determining success. Once this is known the auditor can then ascertain how the process is performing relative to these objectives. If the objectives are not being achieved, then clearly the process is not capable, and the deficiencies may lie in the way the process has been designed or is being managed.

If the process is achieving the objectives, the auditor should proceed to the second question and ascertain whether there is a continual improvement programme in place to improve the way operations are conducted and resources utilized.

If the process is achieving the required results in the best way, the auditor should then proceed to the third question and establish whether the results are, in fact, those needed by the organization to achieve its goals.

If the process is achieving the required results in the best way and the results being achieved are those required by the organization, then the process is being managed effectively.

Process capability

Meaning

Process capability is the inherent ability of a process to reproduce its results consistently during multiple cycles of operation.

ISO 9000 requirements and recommendations

The term 'process capability' is not used in ISO 9001. However, clause 8.2.3 of the standard does require the monitoring and measurement methods to demonstrate the ability of the processes to achieve planned results – which, in other words, is process capability.

Application

In an ideal world, a capable process is one in which all outputs meet the specified requirements. However, there is variation present in every process. A process can be classified into one of four cases:

1 A process is under control and produces product that is acceptable. There is no special cause variation and common cause variation is minimal (process yield is acceptable and predictable).
2 A process is under control and produces product that is acceptable, but there is excessive common cause variation (process yield is unacceptable but predictable).
3 A process can be out of control and produce some product that is acceptable, but also product that is unacceptable due to special cause variation (process yield is unpredictable).
4 A process is out of control and produces no product that is acceptable (process yield is zero).

When the spread of variation is centred on the nominal value of a parameter and the location of the centre does not vary over time, the process is said to be under **statistical control** regardless of the spread of variation. The spread of variation may be so wide and the specification limits so narrow that process yield is very low. In such situations, the process is not capable of producing conforming product consistently. By reducing common cause variation, the spread may be reduced to a level where 99.73 per cent of product meets requirements. This is the three-sigma limit. If variation is reduced even further, so that 99.9999998 per cent of product meets requirements, this is **six-sigma** performance. A process is, therefore, capable if it produces product within agreed limits. For non-manufacturing processes, a level of two sigma (95.45 per cent) may be perfectly acceptable but one sigma (68.26 per cent) is totally unacceptable.

If you operate a ten-stage process and each stage only yields 80 per cent correct output, the total yield would be only 10.7 per cent of the input quantity. So there is significant benefit in increasing the capability of each stage in a process in order to produce more usable output and hence increase process efficiency.

Process control

Meaning

A process is under control when actions induced cause variation in the results. When variations in the results occur by chance, the process is not under control. Therefore, a process that produces unpredictable results is out of control. The spread of variation in results may exceed the limits or the requirements but, if this is predictable, the process is under control. Process control is, therefore, about understanding variation.

ISO 9000 requirements and recommendations

The term 'process control' does not appear in ISO 9000, ISO 9001 or ISO 9004. In its place is the term 'process management', which includes process control.

Application

To bring a process under control, it is necessary to:

1 Determine what parameter is to be controlled.
2 Establish its criticality and whether you need to control before, during or after results are produced.
3 Establish a specification for the parameter to be controlled, which provides limits of acceptability and units of measure.
4 Produce plans for controls that specify the means by which the characteristics will be achieved, and variation detected and removed.
5 Organize resources to implement the plans for **quality control**.
6 Install a sensor at an appropriate point in the process to sense variance from specification.
7 Collect and transmit data to a place for analysis.
8 Verify the results and establish whether the variance is within the range expected for a stable process, where all variation is due to common causes (see **common cause variation**).
9 Diagnose the cause of any variance beyond the expected range – the variation due to special causes (see **special cause variation**).
10 Propose remedies and decide on the action needed to restore the status quo.
11 Take the agreed action and check that process stability has been restored.

Process description

A process description is a set of information that describes the characteristics of a process to a level necessary to enable its effective management.

Process descriptions would include:

- Process objectives.
- Key performance indicators – the indicators by which the achievement of the process objectives will be measured.
- Process owner.
- Process inputs in terms of the materials and information to be processed.
- Process outputs in terms of the products, services and information delivered.
- Set-up and shut down conditions.
- Process flow charts indicating the sequence of actions and decisions identifying those responsible and the interacting processes, actions and references to supporting documentation.
- Resources – physical and human resources required to deliver process outputs.
- Dependencies – the known factors upon which the quality of the process output depends (skills, competencies, behaviours and capabilities).
- Performance measurement methods – measures to detect variation in product and process performance.
- Preventive measures – measures in place to prevent process and product error or failure.

Process management

Meaning

Process management is about managing the activities, resources and behaviours required to achieve a specified objective. An objective will not be achieved by chance – the work required needs to be managed as a process.

ISO 9000 requirements and recommendations

Clause 4 of ISO 9001 requires the processes needed for the quality management system to be managed by the organization in accordance with the requirements of this International Standard.

Application

There is a big difference between operating a process and managing a process. To operate a process, you simply convert inputs into outputs. The inputs may not be adequate, or the outputs may not be what is required or may be inadequate in some way. The equipment, materials and facilities may not be capable, the information and technology may not be dependable, and the people may not be competent. Therefore, to manage a process, one has to manage all the activities, resources and behaviours needed to deliver process objectives.

In order to manage a **process**, there are a number of factors to be determined:

- The process objective.
- How success will be measured.
- The factors affecting success, i.e. what is important.
- The targets for monitoring – whether the success factors are being managed.
- What can jeopardize success – the result of failure modes analysis.
- The key stages in the process to deliver process outputs:
  (a) planning activities – forecasting and acquisition of resources;

(b) preparatory activities on receipt of inputs;
(c) creative activities – innovation, producing, transforming, delivering, etc.;
(d) measurement activities; and
(e) completion activities.
- Provisions put in place to ensure success:
  (a) information management – ensure dependability;
  (b) equipment management – ensure capability;
  (c) people management – ensure competence; and
  (d) measurement management – ensure capability.
- Provisions put in place to prevent failure:
  (a) error proofing;
  (b) automation; and
  (c) supervisor controls.
- Measurement of process outputs.
- Measurement of process efficiency.
- Measurement of process effectiveness.

Process model

A process model is illustrated in ISO 9000, ISO 9001 and ISO 9004 but each model is different. The model in ISO 9000 shows the inputs coming from and going to customers and other interested parties. The model in ISO 9001 shows the inputs coming from and going to customers only. The model in ISO 9004 shows the inputs coming from and going to interested parties.

Customers are interested parties but not all interested parties are customers, therefore, ISO 9000 and ISO 9004 virtually show the same model. It is only from an assessment or

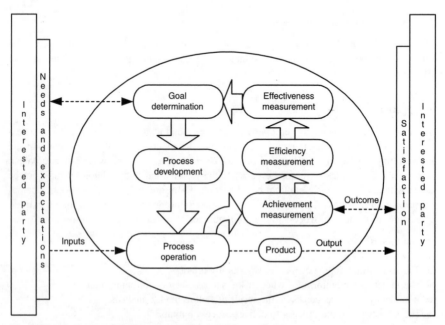

Figure 8   Alternative model of a process based QMS

contractual viewpoint that customer requirements are the focus of the assessment or contract and, therefore, it is this aspect of the quality management system that is being specified and assessed.

These process models of a quality management system are not, in fact, process models at all. They show clauses of the Standard, some of which are not processes. Management responsibility is not a process – it is a collection of requirements. Measurement, analysis and improvement is not a process – these are part of every managed process. An alternative model is illustrated in the figure.

Process parameters

Process parameters are those variables, boundaries or constraints of a process that restrict or determine the results.

Product

A product is anything produced by human effort, natural or man-made processes. In the context of ISO 9000, it is the result of activities or processes.

Product audit

Meaning

A product **audit** is an examination of a process output to determine the extent to which it meets specified requirements.

ISO 9000 requirements and recommendations

There is no specific requirement for a product audit in ISO 9001 but there is a requirement for audits to determine whether the quality management system (QMS) conforms to planned arrangements. The requirements for particular products are planned arrangements and, therefore, the plans made for enabling the organization to satisfy product requirements are part of the QMS and should be audited.

Application

The product audit should establish that:

1 The product requirements have been defined and measures of success established.
2 The provisions needed to accomplish these requirements have been defined.
3 Any changes to the management system processes that are needed to achieve specific product requirements have been identified and effectively communicated.
4 The processes have been modified or new processes designed.
5 The information, resources, criteria and methods for effective operation and control of these processes have been identified, developed and provided.
6 The necessary monitoring, measurement, analysis and improvement processes have been designed and installed.
7 The product plans have been communicated to those concerned.
8 The plans are being implemented as intended.
9 The results being achieved meet the defined requirements.

Product identification

Meaning

Product identification is the act of identifying an entity, i.e. giving it a set of characteristics by which it is recognizable as a member of a group.

ISO 9000 requirements and recommendations

- Clause 7.5.3 of ISO 9001 requires the organization to:
  - (a) identify the product by suitable means throughout **product realization**;
  - (b) identify the product status with respect to monitoring and measurement requirements; and
  - (c) record the unique identification of the product.
- Clause 7.5.4 of ISO 9001 requires the organization to identify customer property provided for use or incorporation into the product.
- Clause 7.5.5 of ISO 9001 requires the organization to identify product as a means of preserving the conformity of product during internal processing and delivery to the intended destination.
- Clause 7.6 of ISO 9001 requires measuring equipment to be identified to enable the calibration status to be determined.
- Clause 8.3 of ISO 9001 requires product that does not conform to product requirements to be identified.

Application

The identification assigned to products or services should enable products and services with one set of characteristics to be distinguishable from products or services with another set of characteristics. Separate product identity is necessary where it is not inherently obvious. If verification is on a go/no go basis, product does not need to be serialized.

If measurements are recorded, some means has to be found of relating the measurements to the product measured. Serial numbers, batch numbers and date codes are suitable means for achieving this. This identity should be carried on all records related to the product.

Product realization

Meaning

All those processes and resources necessary to transform a set of requirements into a product or service that fulfils the requirements.

ISO 9000 requirements and recommendations

- Clause 7.1 of ISO 9001 requires the organization to plan and develop the processes needed for product realization, and planning of product realization be consistent with the requirements of the other processes of the quality management system.
- Clause 8.2.4 of ISO 9001 requires the organization to monitor and measure the characteristics of the product at appropriate stages of the product realization.

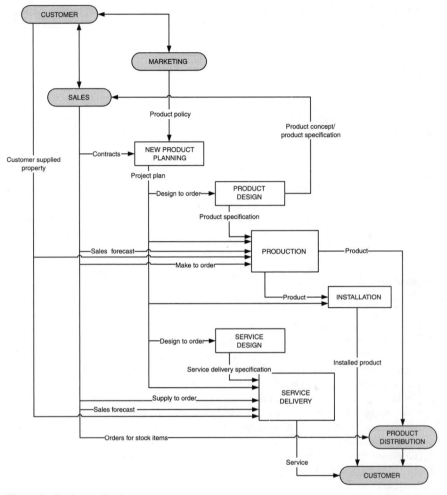

Figure 9   Product realization process

Application

In simple terms the product realization processes are those in the chain from customer order to cash or order fulfilment. Throughout this chain of processes, the product or service is conceived, designed, developed, produced and supplied, and the requirements of the order fulfilled.

Processes that do not act upon or transform the product are not considered product realization processes. A typical product realization process showing the primary subprocesses is illustrated in the figure.

Production

Production is the creation of products. It is one of two principal functions of business – the other is marketing. Marketing is concerned with the determination of customer needs and production is concerned with the satisfaction of those needs. In this sense, production is not a department but a collective term for all the processes that supply the products and services that satisfy customers.

Project audit

Meaning

A project **audit** is an examination of a project, and the associated operations and outputs to determine whether it is being effectively managed.

ISO 9000 requirements and recommendations

There is no specific requirement for a project audit in ISO 9001 but there is a requirement for audits to determine whether the quality management system (QMS) conforms to the planned arrangements. The objectives of particular projects are planned arrangements and, therefore, the plans made for enabling the organization to accomplish project objectives are part of the QMS and, therefore, should be audited.

Application

The project audit should establish that:

1 The project objectives have been defined and measures of success established.
2 The provisions needed to accomplish these objectives have been defined.
3 Any changes to the management system processes that are needed to achieve specific project requirements have been identified and effectively communicated.
4 The processes have been modified or new processes designed.
5 The information, resources, criteria and methods for effective operation and control of these processes have been identified, developed and provided.
6 The necessary monitoring, measurement, analysis and improvement processes have been designed and installed.
7 The project plans have been communicated to those concerned.
8 The plans are being implemented as intended.
9 The results being achieved meet the defined objectives.

Proprietary designs

Proprietary designs are designs exclusively owned by the organization and not sponsored by an external customer.

Prototype

A prototype is a model of a design that is both physically and functionally representative of the design standard for production, and used to verify and validate the design.

Psychological factors of the work environment

Meaning

Psychological factors of the **work environment** are those that arise from an individual's inner needs and external influences, and include recognition, responsibility, achievement, advancement, reward, job security, interpersonal relations, leadership, affiliation, self-esteem and occupational stress. They tend to affect or shape the emotions, feelings, personality, loyalty and attitudes of people and, therefore, the motivation of people towards the job to which they have been assigned.

ISO 9000 requirements and recommendations

Clause 6.4 of ISO 9001 requires the organization to determine and manage the work environment needed to achieve conformity to product requirements. ISO 9000 defines the work environment as a set of conditions under which work is performed and explains that these conditions include **physical**, **social**, psychological and environmental factors.

Application

Managers are often accused of ignoring the human factors, but such factors are not easily identified or managed. With physical factors, you can measure the light level and adjust it if it is too bright or too dim. You cannot measure ethics, **culture**, **climate** or occupational stress – all you see are its effects and the primary effect is employee motivation.

Managers need to understand and analyse human behaviour, and provide conditions in which employees are motivated to achieve the organization's objectives. To do this they need to:

1 Identify and remove job-related barriers – something about the job itself prevents the person performing it from being motivated, e.g. ergonomics, physical conditions, monotony or tedium.
2 Identify and remove goal-related barriers – attainment of the goals is thwarted in some way, e.g. insufficient time, unattainable goals, insufficient physical resources or insufficient competence.
3 Empower employees to achieve objectives by developing their competence, delegating the necessary authority and providing the resources to control the outputs.
4 Measure employee satisfaction in an unbiased manner.

Purchaser

A purchaser is a person or organization that buys from another person or organization. Customers may be purchasers and neither may, in fact, be the users of the product or service being supplied.

Purpose of an organization

Clause 0.1 of ISO 9004 states that the purpose of an organization is to:

- Identify and meet the needs and expectations of its customers and other interested parties (people in the organization, suppliers, owners and society).
- Achieve competitive advantage, and do this in an effective and efficient manner.
- Achieve, maintain and improve overall organizational performance and capabilities.

The purpose statement comprises three elements, the **Vision**, the **Mission** and the **Values**.

Quality

In ISO 9000, quality is defined as the degree to which a set of inherent characteristics fulfils requirements. Requirements are defined in ISO 9000 as a need or expectation that is stated, generally implied or obligatory, therefore, the definition of quality becomes: 'The degree to which a set of inherent characteristics fulfils a need or expectation that is stated, generally implied or obligatory'. Quality is, therefore, a result. It is a noun not an adjective.

In supplying products or services, there are three fundamental parameters that determine their saleability: price, quality and delivery. In producing products and services, there is only one parameter that determines the effectiveness of the processes concerned – it is *quality* judged by the degree to which the processes achieve their objectives. Response, timeliness, economy, productivity and capability are all quality characteristics of a process.

Quality assurance

Quality **assurance**, according to ISO 9000, is part of quality management, focused on providing confidence that quality requirements will be fulfilled. There is a view that quality assurance is about preventing nonconformity, whereas quality control is about detecting it. This may have been how the terms were used in the 1970s but it is no longer valid. Quality assurance is simply about gaining confidence.

Quality control

Quality control is a process for maintaining standards of quality that prevents and corrects change in such standards so that the resultant output meets **customer needs** and **expectations**.

The activities for controlling quality are no different from controlling anything – the only difference is the subject matter (see **control**).

Quality improvement

Quality improvement, according to ISO 9000, is part of quality management focused on increasing the ability to fulfil quality requirements.

There are two types of quality improvement:

● Improvement by better control – this is also called **continual improvement**.
● Improvement by raising standards – this is also called **breakthrough**.

If we want to reduce the common cause variation, we have to act upon the system. If we want to improve efficiency and effectiveness, we also have to act upon the system and both are not concerned with correcting errors, but concerned with doing things better and doing different things.

There is a second dimension to improvement – it is the rate of change. We could improve *gradually* or by a *step change*. Gradual change is also referred to as *incremental improvement*, *continual improvement* or *kaizen*. *Step change* is also referred to as *breakthrough* or a *quantum leap*. Gradual change arises out of refining the existing methods, modifying processes to yield more and more by consuming less and less. Breakthroughs often require innovation, new methods, techniques, technologies and new processes.

Quality management principles

Meaning

A quality management principle is a comprehensive and fundamental rule or belief for assisting an organization in defining, identifying, guiding and validating organizational behaviours. Principles provide guidelines for human conduct that are proven to have enduring, permanent value.

ISO 9000 requirements and recommendations

Clause 0.1 of ISO 9001 states that the quality management principles have been taken into consideration when developing the standard.

Clause 0.2 of ISO 9000 states that eight quality management principles have been identified that can be used by top management in order to lead the organization towards improved performance.

Clause 0.1 of ISO 9004 recommends that the application of quality management principles not only provides direct benefits but also makes an important contribution to managing costs and risks.

Clause 4.3 of ISO 9004 stated that these principles have been developed for use by top management in order to lead the organization toward improved performance.

Application

An organization applies principles. Unlike **values** they are not adopted but if the organization's adopted values do not align with principles, they may prevent it from producing the desired results. The eight quality management principles are identified below and explained further under the respective headings.

Customer focus
Leadership
Involvement of people
Process approach
System approach to management
Continual improvement
Factual approach to decision making
Mutually beneficial supplier relationships

Quality management system

ISO 9000 defines a QMS as a *management system* to direct and control an organization with regard to *quality*. If we insert the ISO 9000 definitions for the words in italics we produce the following *unintelligible* definition: 'A QMS is a set of interrelated or interacting elements that establishes and achieves policy and objectives that direct and control an organization with regard to the degree to which a set of inherent characteristics fulfils requirements'.

A much simpler definition is a set of interconnected processes that enable the organization to achieve its **objectives**. The word 'quality' is superfluous. A better term for this system would be a **business management system** and it is the **business management process** that develops and improves it.

For many years a quality management system has been perceived as a passive set of documents. Documents alone do not achieve results and, therefore, cannot be regarded as a system. For a system to achieve results, it has to comprise dynamic processes that bring resources, activities and behaviours together in the right relationship, and focus effort on the achievement of objectives.

Quality manual

Meaning

ISO 9000 defines a quality manual as a document specifying the quality management system of an organization. It is not intended that the manual be a response to the requirements of ISO 9001. The manual has several uses as:

- A means to communicate the **vision, values, mission, policies** and **objectives** of the organization.
- A means of showing how the system has been designed.
- A means of showing linkages between processes.
- A means of showing who does what.
- An aid to training new people.
- A tool in the analysis of potential improvements.
- A means of demonstrating compliance with external standards and regulations.

For the document to be a manual it needs to be useful. A document that contains no more than a few flow charts will not help people understand how the system operates. If a car maintenance manual contained no more than a diagram of the car, it would not help people maintain the car. Manuals are, as the word implies, documents that provide information for people to do things, such as install, operate, modify and troubleshoot.

ISO 9000 requirements and recommendations

Clause 4.2.2 of ISO 9001 requires the organization to **establish and maintain** a quality manual that includes:

- The scope of the quality management system, including details of and justification for any **exclusions**.
- The documented procedures established for the quality management system, or reference to them.
- A description of the interaction between the processes of the quality management system.

Application

The content of a typical quality manual would include the following.
1 Introduction:

   (a) purpose (of the manual);
   (b) scope (of the manual);

    (c) applicability (of the manual); and

    (d) definitions (of terms used in the manual).

2 Business overview:

    (a) nature of the business/organization – its scope of activity, its products and services;

    (b) the organization's interested parties (customers, employees, regulators, shareholders, suppliers, owners, etc.);

    (c) the context diagram showing the organization relative to its external environment;

    (d) **vision** and **values**;

    (e) **mission**;

    (f) **critical success factors**;

    (g) organization;

    (h) function descriptions;

    (i) organization chart; and

    (j) locations with scope of activity.

3 **Business processes**:

    (a) the system model showing the key business processes and how they are interconnected;

    (b) system performance indicators and method of measurement;

    (c) **business management process** description;

    (d) **resource management process** description;

       (i) physical resources;

       (ii) human resources;

       (iii) financial resources;

    (e) **marketing process** description;

    (f) **order fulfilment process** description;

       (i) sales process;

       (ii) product design process;

       (iii) service design process;

       (iv) production process;

       (v) service delivery;

       (vi) installation process; and

       (vii) distribution process.

4 Function matrix (relationship of functions to processes).

5 Location matrix (relationship of locations to processes).

6 Requirement deployment matrices.

7 ISO 9001 compliance matrix.

8 ISO 14001 compliance matrix.

9 Regulation compliance matrices (Food and Drug Administration (FDA), environment, health, safety, Civil Aviation Authority (CAA), etc.).

10 Approvals (list of current product, process and system approvals and their scope).

Each process would be described in terms of its:

    (a) purpose;

    (b) objectives;

    (c) flow of activities;

    (d) interfaces between other processes;

    (e) competencies and resources required;

    (f) performance measures;

    (g) list of supporting information; and

    (h) list of records indicating activities performed and results of measurements conducted.

Quality objectives

Meaning

Quality **objectives** are those results that the organization needs to achieve in order to improve its ability to meet needs and expectations of all the interested parties.

- Objectives are not policies because objectives, once set, remain until they are achieved, whereas policies, once set, remain until changed.
- If you do not know where you are going, any destination will do!
- To meet customer needs and expectations is a *policy* not an *objective* because it is not something that you achieve then move on to do something else.
- Improving our ability to meet customer needs and expectations is an *objective* not a *policy* because, after setting targets for the level of improvement required, it can be achieved. *Policy* in this area may dictate the manner in which this *ability* is improved.

Quality is defined in ISO 9000 as the degree to which a set of inherent characteristics fulfils requirements. Quality is, therefore, a term that describes the condition of business outcomes. Everything a business does must directly or indirectly affect the condition of its outcomes and, therefore, all business objectives are quality objectives and all quality objectives are business objectives.

ISO 9000 requirements and recommendations

- Clause 4.2.1 of ISO 9001 requires the quality management system documentation to include documented statements of a quality policy and quality objectives.
- Clause 5.1 of ISO 9001 requires top management to provide evidence of its commitment to the development and implementation of the quality management system and continually improve its effectiveness by ensuring that quality objectives are established.
- Clause 5.3 of ISO 9001 requires top management to **ensure** that the quality policy provides a framework for establishing and reviewing quality objectives.
- Clause 5.4.1 of ISO 9001 requires top management to ensure that quality objectives, including those needed to meet requirements for product, are established at relevant functions and levels within the organization, and that the quality objectives are measurable and consistent with the quality policy.
- Clause 5.4.2 of ISO 9001 requires top management to ensure that the planning of the quality management system is carried out in order to meet the requirements given in 4.1, as well as the quality objectives.
- Clause 5.6.1 of ISO 9001 requires top management to review the organization's quality management system, at planned intervals, to assess opportunities for improvement and the need for changes to quality objectives.
- Clause 6.2.2 of ISO 9001 requires the organization to ensure that its personnel are aware of the relevance and importance of their activities, and how they contribute to the achievement of the quality objectives.
- Clause 7.1 of ISO 9001 requires the organization to determine the quality objectives and requirements for the product.
- Clause 8.5.1 of ISO 9001 requires the organization to improve the effectiveness of the quality management system continually through the use of the quality objectives.

Application

To establish any objective:

- Define the purpose or mission of the entity to which the objective is related – the organization, a process, a task, a product or a service.
- Assemble a group of people who have a vested interest in fulfilling this purpose.
- Ask the question 'What affects our ability to fulfil this purpose/mission?'.
- Collect the answers, group under categories and simplify. The result is a set of **critical success factors** and hence subjects for which objectives are necessary.
- Use **SMART** to help write the objective.

Objectives may be set at different levels addressing different factors, for example:

- Corporate level, which addresses image, profitability and growth.
- Process level, which addresses **process capability**, efficiency and effectiveness, use of resources, and controllability.
- Product level, which addresses the identified needs and expectations of customers, in both the elimination of errors and provision of product features that satisfy needs.
- Departmental level, which addresses the capability, efficiency and effectiveness of the organization, its responsiveness to change, the environment in which people work, etc.
- Personnel level, which addresses the skills, knowledge, ability, competency, motivation and development of people.

The objective setting process consists of the following stages:

1 Identify the need.
2 Draft preliminary objectives.
3 Define the measures that will indicate the objective has been achieved.
4 Prove the need to the appropriate level of management in terms of:
   (a) whether the climate for change is favourable;
   (b) the urgency of the improvement or controls;
   (c) the size of the losses or potential losses;
   (d) the priorities.
5 Identify or set up the forum where the question of change or control is discussed.
6 Conduct a feasibility study to establish whether the objective can be achieved with the resources that can be applied.
7 Validate the objectives using **SMART**.
8 Communicate the objectives.

Quality planning

Meaning

Quality planning involves the provisions made to achieve the needs and expectations of an organization's interested parties and prevent failure.

ISO 9000 defines quality planning as part of quality management focused on setting quality objectives and specifying necessary operational processes and related resources to fulfil the quality objectives.

ISO 9000 requirements and recommendations

Clause 5.4.2 of ISO 9004 recommends that management should take responsibility for the quality planning of the organization. This planning should focus on defining the processes needed to meet the organization's quality objectives and requirements effectively and efficiently, consistent with the strategy of the organization.

Application

As quality is defined as the degree to which a set of inherent characteristics fulfils requirements, it follows that *all* planning is quality planning. One plans only to achieve an objective – a requirement that can be of one's own making or imposed by **interested parties**. In this context there would be plans at corporate, departmental, process, project, product, service and personnel levels.

Quality plans

Quality plans define how specified **quality requirements** will be achieved, controlled, assured and managed for specific contracts, projects or products. They specify the processes of the quality management system (including the **product realization** processes) and the resources to be applied to a specific product, project or contract.

Sometimes the project is so complex that separate plans may be needed simply to separate the subject matter into digestible chunks. The disadvantage in giving any document a label with the word *quality* in the title is that it can sometimes be thought of as a document that serves only the quality department rather than a document that defines the provisions for managing the various processes that will be utilized on the project. The content of the plans depend upon the work that is required and, therefore, may include:

- project plans;
- product development plans;
- production plans;
- procurement plans;
- reliability and maintainability programme plans;
- control plans or verification plans;
- installation plans;
- commissioning plans; and
- performance evaluation plans.

Quality policy

Meaning

ISO 9000 defines quality **policy** as the overall intentions and direction of an organization related to quality as formally expressed by top management. The quality policy exists to shape behaviour and establishes the core values in an organization and, therefore, equates with the corporate policy.

ISO 9000 requirements and recommendations

- Clause 4.2.1 of ISO 9001 requires the quality management system documentation to include documented statements of a quality policy.
- Clause 5.1 of ISO 9001 requires top management to provide evidence of its commitment to the development and implementation of the quality management system, and continually improve its effectiveness by establishing the quality policy.
- Clause 5.3 of ISO 9001 requires that top management **ensure** that the quality policy:

(a) is appropriate to the **purpose of the organization**;

(b) includes a commitment to comply with requirements and continually improve the effectiveness of the quality management system;

(c) provides a framework for establishing and reviewing quality objectives;

(d) is communicated and understood within the organization; and

(e) is reviewed for continuing suitability.

- Clause 5.4.1 of ISO 9001 requires the quality objectives to be measurable and consistent with the quality policy.
- Clause 5.6.1 of ISO 9001 requires the management review to assess the need for changes to the quality management system, including the quality policy.
- Clause 8.5.1 of ISO 9001 requires the organization to improve the effectiveness of the quality management system continually through the use of the quality policy.

Application

Policies are not expressed as vague statements or emphatic statements using the words *may*, *should* or *shall*. They express clear intentions by using the words *we will*, expressing a commitment, or by the words *we are, we do, we don't, we have*, expressing shared beliefs. In the ISO 9000:2000 definition of quality policy, it is suggested that the eight quality management principles be used as a basis for establishing the policy. Examples of corporate policies using these principles are as follows.

- On customers: 'We will listen to our customers, understand and balance their needs and expectations with those of our suppliers, employees, investors and society and endeavour to give full satisfaction to all parties'.
- On leadership: 'We will establish and communicate our vision for the organization and through our leadership exemplify core values to guide the behaviour of all to achieve our vision'.
- On people: 'We will involve our people in the organization's development, utilize their knowledge and experience, recognize their contribution and provide an environment in which they are motivated to realize their full potential'.
- On processes and systems: 'We will take a process approach towards the management of work and manage our processes as a single system of interconnected processes that delivers all the organization's objectives'.
- On continual improvement: 'We will provide an environment in which every person is motivated continually to improve the efficiency and effectiveness of our products, processes and our management system'.
- On decisions: 'We will base our decisions on the logical and intuitive analysis of data collected where possible from accurate measurements of product, process and system characteristics'.
- On supplier relationships: 'We will develop alliances with our suppliers and work with them jointly to improve performance'.

Quality requirements

Quality requirements are those requirements that pertain to the features and characteristics of a product or service that are required to be fulfilled in order to satisfy a given need.

ISO 9000 is often perceived as a quality requirement. It is, but only in so far that it is a requirement that applies to a management system. Other standards, specifications or regulations are also quality requirements. Therefore, if one were to list all the quality requirements that applied to a product, one would list all the documents that specified requirements that related to the product, not simply ISO 9000.

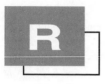

Records

Meaning

ISO 9000 defines a record as a document stating results achieved or providing evidence of activities performed.

ISO 9000 requirements and recommendations

- Clause 4.2.1 of ISO 9001 requires the quality management system documentation to include records required by this International Standard.
- Clause 4.2.3 of ISO 9001 requires records to be controlled according to the requirements given in clause 4.2.4.
- Clause 4.2.4 of ISO 9001 requires records to be established and maintained to provide evidence of conformity to requirements and of the effective operation of the quality management system.
- Clause 4.2.4 of ISO 9001 requires records to remain legible, readily identifiable and retrievable, and that a documented procedure be established to define the controls needed for the identification, storage, protection, retrieval, retention time and disposition of records.
- Clause 5.6.1 of ISO 9001 requires records from management reviews to be maintained.
- Clause 6.2.2 of ISO 9001 requires appropriate records of education, training, skills and experience to be maintained.
- Clause 7.1 of ISO 9001 requires the records needed to provide evidence that the realization processes and resulting product fulfil requirements to be determined.
- Clause 7.2.2 of ISO 9001 requires records of the results of the review of requirements relating to product and actions arising from the review to be maintained.
- Clause 7.3.2 of ISO 9001 requires records of design inputs to be maintained.
- Clause 7.3.2 of ISO 9001 requires records of the results of design and development reviews to be maintained.
- Clause 7.3.5 of ISO 9001 requires records of the results of design and development verification and any necessary actions to be maintained.
- Clause 7.3.6 of ISO 9001 requires records of the results of design and development validation and any necessary actions to be maintained.
- Clause 7.3.7 of ISO 9001 requires records of the review of design and development changes and any necessary actions to be maintained.
- Clause 7.4.1 of ISO 9001 requires records of the results of supplier evaluations and any necessary actions arising from the evaluation to be maintained.

- Clause 7.5.2 of ISO 9001 requires the organization to establish requirements for process records to be maintained.
- Clause 7.5.3 of ISO 9001 requires the organization to record the unique identification of the product where **traceability** is a requirement.
- Clause 7.5.4 of ISO 9001 requires records maintained of any **customer property** that is lost, damaged or otherwise found to be unsuitable for use.
- Clause 7.6 of ISO 9001 requires the basis used for calibration or verification to be recorded where no such standards exist.
- Clause 7.6 of ISO 9001 requires the organization to assess and record the validity of the previous measuring results when the equipment is found not to conform to requirements.
- Clause 7.6 of ISO 9001 requires records of the results of calibration and verification to be maintained.
- Clause 8.2.2 of ISO 9001 requires the responsibilities and requirements for maintaining records of internal audits shall be defined in a documented procedure.
- Clause 8.2.2 of ISO 9001 requires records to indicate the person(s) authorizing release of product.
- Clause 8.3 of ISO 9001 requires records of the nature of nonconformities and any subsequent actions taken, including concessions obtained, to be maintained.
- Clause 8.5.2 of ISO 9001 requires a documented procedure to be established to define requirements for records of the results of corrective action taken.
- Clause 8.5.3 of ISO 9001 requires a documented procedure to be established to define requirements for records of the results of preventive action taken.

Application

Records have a life cycle. Once they are generated, they acquire an identity and are then assigned for storage for a prescribed period. During use and storage they need to be protected from inadvertent or malicious destruction. They need to be brought out of storage quickly to support current activities or investigations. When their usefulness has lapsed, a decision is made as to whether to retain them further or to destroy them.

You need to carry out the following actions.

- Identify the records that specify results achieved and activities performed:
  (a) where results are needed or make acceptance decisions – you need to know what you achieved so that you can decide if it meets the requirement;
  (b) where results are needed to evaluate performance – you need to know what you achieved so that you can determine if your objectives are being achieved;
  (c) where knowledge of activities is necessary to perform subsequent activities – you need to know what you did so that you can determine what else you should do;
  (d) where knowledge of activities is necessary to investigate performance – you need to know what you did so that you can discover what went wrong and find the root cause.
- Indicate the records to be produced and maintained in the procedures that address the related activities.
- Keep records up to date.
- Keep the information in the records up to date.
- Keep the records in good condition.
- Give each record a reference number and a name or title in a prominent location on the record in order to determine what it is, what kind of information it records and what it relates to.

- Enable authorized retrieval of records and prohibit unauthorized retrieval.
- Do not store company records in personal files.
- Index records to ensure that you have all the records that have been produced and that none are missing.
- Protect records as appropriate against loss by fire, theft, unauthorized removal, loss through computer viruses and unauthorized access, deletion or their corruption.
- Do not destroy records before their useful life is over. Factors to consider are:
  (a) the duration of the contract;
  (b) the life of the product; and
  (c) the period between management system assessments.

Registrar

A registrar is an organization that is authorized to certify organizations. The body may be accredited or non-accredited.

Registration

Registration is a process of recording details of organizations of assessed capability that have satisfied prescribed standards. (See also **certification body**.)

Regulator

A regulator is a legal body authorized to enforce compliance with the laws and statutes of a national government.

Regulatory requirements

Regulatory requirements are requirements established by law pertaining to organizations, products or services.

Relevant authorities

Meaning

A relevant authority is a person or organization that is recognized by the community in which they operate as authorized to make certain decisions and has a vested interest in the outcome.

ISO 9000 requirements and recommendations

- Clause 8.2.4 of ISO 9001 requires the organization to deal with nonconforming product, when appropriate, by authorizing its use, release or acceptance under concession by a relevant authority.
- Clause 8.2.4 of ISO 9001 requires uncompleted product or service delivery not to proceed to release unless approved by a relevant authority.

Application

The relevant authority to which you would offer a nonconforming or uncompleted product for acceptance might be the customer, the designer, the regulator or an internal acceptance authority. You would not seek acceptance from someone or some organization that had no interest in the outcome, whether or not they were competent to make such decisions.

Remedial action

Remedial action is action proposed or taken to remove a nonconformity. (See also **corrective action** and **preventive action**.)

Requirement of the standard

A sentence containing the word 'shall'. N.B. Some sentences contain multiple requirements, such as to 'establish', 'document' and 'maintain'. This is, in fact, three requirements.

Resource management

Meaning

Resource management is one of the core **business processes**. It is a series of processes that determine, acquire, deploy and maintain the resources needed to meet the organization's objectives and dispose of those resources that are no longer required.

Resources include anything of which there is an available supply, such as physical, financial and human assets, and, therefore, include equipment, plant, machinery, buildings, land, space, energy, materials, money and people. They can also include knowledge, as specialist knowledge may exist in the outside world that needs to be acquired for use in the organization. Time is also a resource when allocated or wasted in connection with the execution of work. Human resources include management, professional and operational personnel as well as contractors and temporary staff.

ISO 9000 requirements and recommendations

- Clause 4.1 of ISO 9001 requires the organization to **ensure** the availability of resources.
- Clause 5.1 of ISO 9001 requires top management to provide evidence of its commitment to the development and implementation of the quality management system and continually improve its effectiveness by ensuring the availability of resources.
- Clause 5.6.3 of ISO 9001 requires the output from the management review to include any decisions and actions related to resource needs.
- Clause 6.1 of ISO 9001 requires the organization to determine and provide the resources needed to implement and maintain the quality management system, continually improve its effectiveness, and to enhance **customer satisfaction** by meeting customer requirements.
- Clause 7.1 of ISO 9001 requires the organization to determine the need to provide resources specific to the product.

Application

There are departments that are perceived to manage resources, such as the finance department, the calibration department, the purchasing department and the maintenance department, but each only performs part of the process necessary to manage these resources.

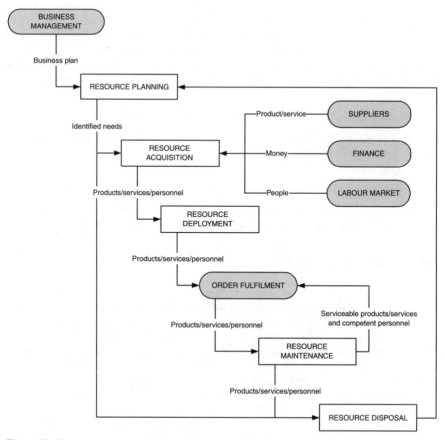

Figure 10   Resource management process

Although resources are required to market, design, sell, produce, deliver and install product, the processes concerned with these activities simply utilize a resource that is provided by another process. The human resource management process delivers competent personnel to the production process even though staff in this process may select and train the personnel. The equipment maintenance process delivers serviceable equipment to the production process even though staff in the production department may perform equipment maintenance.

There are five separate processes within resource management as illustrated in the figure. Each of the five processes may be subdivided into one or more subprocesses depending on whether they are physical, financial or human resources.

Responsibility and authority

Meaning

Responsibility is, in simple terms, an area in which one is entitled to act on one's own accord and is commonly used informally to imply an obligation. **Authority** is, in simple terms, the right to take actions and make decisions.

It is necessary for management to define who should do what in order that the designated work is assigned to competent personnel to be carried out and that the effort to perform it is optimized appropriately.

In the absence of the delegation of authority and assignment of responsibilities:

- Individuals assume duties that may duplicate those duties assumed by others.
- Jobs that are necessary but unattractive would be left undone.
- Work may be performed by personnel who are not competent, thus jeopardizing the ability of the organization to meet its objectives.

ISO 9000 requirements and recommendations

Clause 5.5.1 of ISO 9001 requires top management to ensure that the responsibilities and authorities are defined and communicated within the organization.

Application

When it has been decided what is to be done, the next task is to decide who shall do it. Work should be performed only by those competent to execute it. Responsibility should not be assigned without the authority to control the results also being delegated.

- Use organization structure diagrams to define and communicate positions and relationships.
- Use function descriptions to define and communicate the purpose and role of each function in the organization.
- Use job or role descriptions to define and communicate the responsibilities and authority of individuals.
- Use procedures to define and communicate where, when and what actions and decisions the functions, roles or positions are to perform.
- Ensure that staff account for their actions and decisions, so as to confirm they are exercising their duties responsibly.
- Remember that authority is passed downward within the organization and divided among subordinate personnel, whereas responsibility passes upwards, hence managers remain responsible for the subordinates' use of delegated authority.
- Responsibility for results rests with those who stipulate the course of action.
- It is better to give personnel an objective to achieve, provide them with the training to perform the job competently and then let them decide how they will achieve the objective.

Review

Meaning

To review means to take another look at something. However, ISO 9000 defines a review as an activity undertaken to determine the suitability, adequacy and effectiveness of the subject matter to achieve established objectives. A review in the context of ISO 9000 is, therefore, a lot more than another look at something but a planned event designed to establish whether something remains fit for its purpose.

ISO 9000 requirements and recommendations

- Clause 4.2.3 of ISO 9001 requires a documented procedure to be established to define the controls needed to review documents.
- Clause 5.1 of ISO 9001 requires top management to provide evidence of its commitment to the development and implementation of the quality management system, and continually improve its effectiveness by conducting management reviews.
- Clause 5.3 of ISO 9001 requires top management to ensure that the quality policy provides a framework for establishing and reviewing quality objectives.
- Clause 5.3 of ISO 9001 requires the quality policy to be reviewed for continuing suitability.
- Clause 5.6.1 of ISO 9001 requires top management to review the organization's quality management system, at planned intervals.
- Clause 7.2.2 of ISO 9001 requires the organization to review the requirements related to the product.
- Clause 7.3.1 of ISO 9001 requires the organization to determine the reviews appropriate to each design and development stage during the design and development planning.
- Clause 7.3.2 of ISO 9001 requires design and development inputs to be reviewed for adequacy.
- Clause 7.3.4 of ISO 9001 requires systematic reviews of design and development to be conducted in accordance with planned arrangements at suitable stages.
- Clause 7.3.7 of ISO 9001 requires design and development changes to be reviewed, before implementation.
- Clause 7.5.2 of ISO 9001 requires defined criteria for review and approval of processes.
- Clause 8.5.2 of ISO 9001 requires a documented procedure to be established to define requirements for reviewing nonconformities and corrective action taken.
- Clause 8.5.3 of ISO 9001 requires a documented procedure to be established to define requirements for reviewing preventive action taken.

Application

Reviews should be planned and be conducted against defined criteria so as to provide a basis for objectivity. It is not necessary that the reviews be conducted by personnel different to those who produced the results being reviewed, but often independence does provide for greater objectivity. If operations continue without periodic review, there is a tendency for them to become less relevant, for errors to escape detection and for actions to be overlooked. Periodic reviews in all operations keep the organization alert to changes that may jeopardize its success.

Revision status

Meaning

When a document is revised its status changes to signify that it is no longer identical to the original version.

ISO 9000 requirements and recommendations

Clause 4.2.3 of ISO 9001 requires the organization to define the controls needed to ensure that the current revision status of documents is identified.

Application

Revision status may be indicated by date, by letter or by number, or may be a combination of issue and revision. Every change to a document should revise the revision index. Issue 1 may denote the original version. Upon changing the document, an incremental change to the revision index is made so that the new version is now issue 2 or issue 1.1 depending on the convention adopted.

Roles

Meaning

A role is a set of expectations and obligations to act in a specific way in certain contexts.

The term 'role' can be ascribed to an individual or a group of individuals. It is also used to ascribe a purpose to inanimate objects, such as the role of statistical techniques (clause 2.10 of ISO 9000). In general, 'role' is one of several terms used to describe what people do at any given time. For example, a quality manager in an engineering company, chairing a meeting on quality improvement has a profession, an occupation, a job, a position and a role.

- The profession is *engineering,* for which there are numerous occupations.
- The occupation is *quality management*, for which there are several positions.
- The position is *quality manager*, which comprises several jobs.
- The job is *change management*, which embraces a number of roles.
- The role is *leader* at this point in time.

An illustration of how the roles change is given in the following. The quality manager collects data to reveal facts. The role changes from leader to analyst. Later the quality manager takes the facts and searches for causes. The role changes from analyst to investigator. After finding the causes, the quality manager encourages others to produce solutions – the role is now facilitator. If the quality manager produced the solutions, the role undertaken would be designer or innovator. Once the problems are solved, the quality manager goes to see the customer to show how performance has improved. The role changes again – this time to ambassador.

In another context this quality manager may be a mother of three children, a director of a local drama group and a freedom fighter for justice in the local community. All are roles.

All these roles for some people are jobs because they perform them continuously. For others, they are transitory.

ISO 9000 requirements and recommendations

- Clause 2.6 of ISO 9004 recommends that the role of top management is to create an environment where people are fully involved and in which a quality management system can operate effectively.
- Clause 2.8.3 of ISO 9004 recommends that one role of top management is to carry out regular systematic evaluations of the suitability, adequacy, effectiveness and efficiency of the quality management system with respect to the quality policy and quality objectives.
- The term 'role' is not used in ISO 9001.
- Clause 5.2.3 of ISO 9004 recommends that consideration should also be given to the role of the organization in the protection of community interests.

Application

People should undertake roles commensurate with their skills and competencies. This is why a person in the position of quality manager may not be the right person to undertake the role of change agent, ambassador or project leader.

Whatever the positions and jobs people occupy, it is their roles that are important. The key is to define what roles are required to achieve an objective. If the object is to put on the play, *Romeo and Juliet* by William Shakespeare, there are several roles to fill. Those selected for each role are chosen for their ability to play the part as the bard intended. Simply because they are actors does not mean they can play every part effectively!

Second-party audit

A second-party **audit** is an audit performed by a customer upon its suppliers.

Self-assessment

Meaning

Self-assessment is a process of determining the degree to which an organization meets certain criteria. It is performed by the organization upon itself to identify opportunities for improvement.

ISO 9004 defines self-assessment as a carefully considered evaluation resulting in an opinion or judgement of the effectiveness and efficiency of the organization, and the maturity of the quality management system.

ISO 9000 requirements and recommendations

There is no requirement for self-assessment in ISO 9001, but ISO 9004 recommends that self-assessment can provide an overall view of the performance of the organization and the degree of maturity of the quality management system, thus assisting in the identification of areas requiring improvement.

Application

Self-assessment may be performed against any set of criteria but to have value to the interested parties, the criteria needs to be accepted by them as being of a recognized standard. Thus an organization examining its operations against ISO 9001, ISO 9004 or the European Foundation for Quality Management (EFQM) Business Excellence criteria is a self-assessment.

Six sigma

The Greek letter σ called 'sigma' is the symbol used to represent standard deviation – a measure of the spread of frequency distributions. It is the root mean square deviation of the readings in a series from their average value. Six sigma is, therefore, six standard deviations.

In a perfect world, we would like the range of variation to be well within the upper and lower specification limits for the characteristics being measured but invariably we produce defectives. If there were an 80 per cent yield from each stage in a ten-stage process, the resultant output would be less than 11 per cent and as indicated in the first table.

Stage	Yield/stage	Total percentage yield	Initial population: one million
1	0.80	80	800 000.00
2	0.80	64	512 000.00
3	0.80	51.2	262 144.00
4	0.80	41	107 374.18
5	0.80	32.8	35 184.37
6	0.80	26.2	9 223.37
7	0.80	21	1 934.28
8	0.80	16.8	324.52
9	0.80	13.4	43.56
10	0.80	10.7	4.68

We would obtain only four good products from an initial batch of one million. Even if the process stage yield was 99 per cent, we would still only obtain half of the products we started with. It is, therefore, essential that multiple stage processes have a process stage yield well in excess of 99 per cent and it is from this perspective that the concept of six sigma emerges. The process yield at various sigma values is given in the second table.

Sigma	Percentage of product meeting requirements	Number of nonconformities per million products	ppm (assuming 1.5 sigma drift)
1	68.26	317 400	697 672.15
2	95.45	45 500	308 770.21
3	99.73	2 700	66 810.63
4	99.993 7	63	6 209.70
5	99.999 943	0.57	232.67
6	99.999 999 8	0.002	3.4

Social factors of the work environment

Meaning

Social factors of the **work environment** are those that arise from interactions between people and include the impact of an individual's family, education, religion and peer pressure as well as the impact of the organization's ethics, **culture and climate**.

ISO 9000 requirements and recommendations

Clause 6.4 of ISO 9001 requires the organization to determine and manage the work environment needed to achieve conformity to product requirements. ISO 9000 defines the work environment as a set of conditions under which work is performed and explains that these conditions include **physical**, social, **psychological** and **environmental factors**.

Application

Social interaction between people is vital for many people to enjoy their work. People require affection, affiliation, acknowledgement, recognition and the opportunity to exchange ideas. Isolation is only suitable for a few. Social interaction can be a motivating force in an organization but can also lead to friction that affects worker performance. In managing the social factors of the work environment, the manager needs to understand the need for people to communicate with others and understand the social factors that can impede performance. For example:

- Being aware of a person's social needs and being sensitive to meeting these needs.
- Identifying the behavioural profile of a person, i.e. whether they are analyticals, drivers, amiables or expressives:
  (a) Analyticals focus on facts, on detail, on the past and are cautious. They make good troubleshooters but dislike involvement with others.
  (b) Amiables focus on relationships, seek opinions and consensus. They make good co-ordinators and counsellors, but dislike interpersonal conflict.
  (c) Drivers focus on action and results. They make good leaders but dislike inaction.
  (d) Expressives focus on the future, the big picture. They make good innovators but dislike being alone.
- Being aware of the social environment into which a person is to be placed before placement.
- Providing training in teambuilding so that personnel become more confident when working with their colleagues.
- Choosing as the leader someone who exhibits the characteristics of leadership – not someone who is more comfortable working alone.
- Taking prompt action on finding adverse social interaction in the workplace.
- Operating an 'open door' policy that encourages personnel to air their grievances without fear of being ridiculed.

Special cause variation

Special cause **variation** is a cause of variation that can be assigned to a specific or special condition that does not apply to other events.

A stable process is one with no indication of a special cause of variation and can be said to be in **statistical control**. Special cause variation is not random – it is unpredictable. It occurs because something has happened that should not have happened, so you should search for the cause immediately and eliminate it. They are causes that are not always present. The wrong material, an inaccurate measuring device, a worn-out tool, a sick employee, the weather conditions, an accident, a stage omitted – these are all one-off events that cannot be predicted. Eliminating the special causes is part of **quality control** – taking **corrective action** to prevent the recurrence of a problem.

Stakeholder

A stakeholder is a person or organization that has the freedom to provide something to or withdraw something from an enterprise. For example:

- Customers are stakeholders because they can withdraw their custom, i.e. take their business elsewhere.

- Employees are stakeholders because they can withdraw their labour, i.e. leave the organization for a job elsewhere.
- Suppliers are stakeholders because they can refuse or terminate the supply of products or services.
- Investors are stakeholders because they can withdraw their investment.
- Society is a stakeholder because it can cause laws to be changed or enforced that make organizations cease the practices that offend society.

Statistical control

Statistical control is a condition of a process in which there is no indication of a special cause of variation. All variation is due to common cause. A process may be under statistical control and continue to produce nonconforming product. The difference between a process that is under statistical control and one that is not is that its performance is predictable and stable.

Status and importance in auditing

Meaning

Status has three meanings in the context of ISO 9000:

1 The relative position of the process or area in the scheme of things.
2 The maturity of the process.
3 The performance of the process.

The importance of a process is its significance relative to the needs of interested parties and the relative influence of these interested parties.

ISO 9000 requirements and recommendations

Clause 8.2.2 of ISO 9001 requires the **audit programme** to be planned, taking into consideration the status and importance of the processes and areas to be audited.

Application

Select processes firstly on the basis of importance and secondly on the basis of status. The status and importance of the activities will determine whether the audit is scheduled once a month, once a year or left for three years – any longer and the activity might be considered to have no value in the organization.

Customers are the most influential and, therefore, the processes in the chain from identification of needs to satisfaction of those needs are the most important. Processes that serve the protection of the environment may be considered more important in some industries where the environmental impacts are more significant. For instance, in the chemical industry, giving greater priority to customer facing processes than environmental facing processes might result in there being no customers at all if the plant is closed down due to breach of environmental legislation.

Important processes that exhibit poor performance relative to their achievement of objectives should be targeted more often than important processes that perform as intended.

Strategic audit

Meaning

A strategic **audit** is an examination of the arrangements made to accomplish the mission of the organization.

ISO 9000 requirements and recommendations

There is no specific requirement for a strategic audit in ISO 9001 but there is a requirement for audits to determine that the quality management system conforms to the planned arrangements. The organization's purpose and mission are planned arrangements. The strategic objectives and plans made for enabling the organization to accomplish its mission are part of the quality management system and, therefore, should be audited.

Application

The strategic audit should establish that:

1 There is a defined process for establishing the organization's goals and objectives.
2 An analysis of current and future needs of customers and other interested parties has been carried out.
3 The requirements that the organization needs to meet to fulfil its mission have been determined.
4 Objectives have been established for achieving these requirements.
5 Priorities for action have been set.
6 The products, services and projects that need to be developed or abandoned to achieve these objectives have been identified.
7 The risks to success have been quantified.
8 The processes for achieving the objectives have been designed and constructed.
9 The information, resources, criteria and methods for effective operation of these processes have been identified, developed and provided.
10 The necessary monitoring, measurement, analysis and improvement processes have been designed and installed.
11 The strategic plans have been deployed to those concerned.
12 The plans are being implemented as intended.
13 The results being achieved meet the strategic objectives.

Subcontract requirements

Subcontract requirements are requirements placed on a subcontractor that are derived from the requirements of a main **contract**.

Subcontractor

A subcontractor is a person or organization that enters into a **contract** in which some of the obligations of the prime contractor are stipulated. Subcontractors extend the capability of a prime contractor. They differ from suppliers in that they provide products and services to customer specifications, whereas suppliers provide products and services to their own specifications.

Supplier assessment

Supplier assessment is an activity performed to determine the capability of a supplier to meet certain criteria. Supplier assessments are performed for a number of reasons:

- To select a credible supplier for a future purchase.
- To select a supplier for a specific purchase.
- To verify continued capability of an existing supplier.

There are several parts to supplier assessments, each focusing on some aspect of required performance:

- *Technical assessment* – for checking the products, processes or services to establish they are what the supplier claims them to be.
- *Quality system assessment* – for checking the certification status of the quality system, verifying that any certification was properly accredited.
- *Financial assessment* – for checking the credit rating, insurance risk, stability, etc.
- *Ethical assessment* – for checking probity, conformance with professional standards and codes.

System

A system is a chain of interconnected components or processes that produce strategic results. All the components or processes work in harmony to achieve the stated goals. A system has many components or processes, each of which has a unique purpose within the system but without which the system cannot function.

Systems break down when one or more of these components or processes fail to fulfil their purpose. For example, a transport system provides a capability for users to move goods and people quickly and safely to their chosen destination. If the trains break down, the system breaks down because the buses have not been designed to carry the load of road and rail travellers. If a process is designed or changed so that its objectives are not aligned with those of the system, the system will also fail. For example, the finance department decides to delay paying suppliers in order to meet financial targets. Suppliers get annoyed and terminate supply of product. Production stops and the customer becomes dissatisfied. This leads to the formation of a **system approach** to management. Another example is shown in **audit scope**.

System approach

The system approach to management is one of the eight quality management principles used as a basis for developing ISO 9000. The principle is expressed as follows: 'Identifying, understanding and managing interrelated processes as a system contributes to the organization's effectiveness and efficiency in achieving its objectives'.

An organization applying the system approach principle would be one in which people are:

- Defining the organization as a system that is established to achieve **organizational goals**.
- Defining the system by identifying or developing the processes that affect a given objective.
- Structuring the system to achieve the objective in the most efficient and effective way.

- Understanding the interdependencies among the processes of the system.
- Continually improving the system through measurement and evaluation.
- Establishing resource constraints prior to action so that **system integrity** is maintained when changes are made.

System audit

Meaning

A system **audit** is an audit carried out to establish whether a management system conforms to a prescribed standard or meets defined objectives in both its design and its implementation.

ISO 9000 requirements and recommendations

The term 'system audit' is not used in ISO 9001 or ISO 9004. In ISO 9000, audits of the organization's management system against the organization's management system requirements or the requirements of International Standards, such as ISO 9001 and ISO 14001:1996, are referred to as management system audits.

Application

System audits should be designed to verify that the system is capable of:

- Implementing the agreed policies (a **policy audit**).
- Enabling the organization to achieve the agreed objectives (a **strategic audit**).
- Enabling the organization to meet specific product requirements (a **project audit** or **product audit**).

System effectiveness

Meaning

System effectiveness is the ability of a system to achieve its stated purpose and objectives. (See also **Effectiveness of the system.**)

ISO 9000 requirements and recommendations

- Clause 5.3 of ISO 9001 requires top management to ensure that the quality policy includes a commitment to improve the effectiveness of the quality management system continually.
- Clause 5.5.3 of ISO 9001 requires top management to ensure that communication takes place regarding the effectiveness of the quality management system.
- Clause 5.6.3 of ISO 9001 requires the output from the management review to include any decisions and actions related to improvement of the effectiveness of the quality management system.
- Clause 8.1 of ISO 9001 requires the organization to plan and implement the monitoring, measurement, analysis and improvement processes needed to improve the effectiveness of the quality management system continually.
- Clause 8.5.1 of ISO 9001 requires the organization to improve the effectiveness of the quality management system continually.

Application

In the past it has been assumed that, if people were found to be following the procedures as documented, the system was effective. But this was not the reason for the system, i.e. it was not the purpose of the system to force people to follow procedures. The purpose was to ensure results. A system is, therefore, effective only if it can be demonstrated that the desired results are being achieved. But what are the desired results? Is the desired result simply conformity with ISO 9001 or is this just a by-product? It is suggested that conformity with ISO 9001 is not a desired result but a desirable outcome. System effectiveness is, therefore, not measured on whether conformity with ISO 9001 could be demonstrated but on whether the system causes the needs and expectations of the interested parties to be satisfied – the real reason why the system exists.

In order to determine system effectiveness, it is, therefore, necessary to:

1 Identify the needs and expectations of the **interested parties**.
2 Determine the quantifiable targets for these needs and expectations so as to enable their measurement.
3 Identify the data that need to be collected to measure achievement of the targets.
4 Install in the relevant process the means to collect the data.
5 Collect and analyse the data.
6 Determine whether the predefined targets have been achieved – the gap is the measure of effectiveness.

System integrity

Meaning

The system can be described in four different ways.

1 The *manifest* condition – the system as formally described and displayed. This condition may be expressed in manuals, procedures, policies, charts, etc.
2 The *assumed* condition – the system as it is assumed to be by the individual concerned. This condition may be revealed by observation of individuals in action, the decisions they take or listening to how they talk about the system.
3 The *extant* condition – the system as revealed by systematic exploration and analysis. This condition may be revealed by internal or external audit.
4 The *requisite* condition – the system as it would have to be to accord with the real properties of the field in which it exists.

The integrity of the quality management system is the degree to which the manifest, assumed, extant and requisite systems are in harmony.

ISO 9000 requirements and recommendations

Clause 5.4.2 of ISO 9001 requires top management to ensure that the integrity of the quality management system is maintained when changes to the quality management system are planned and implemented.

Application

To maintain the integrity of the management system, you need to do the following:

● Make sure the descriptions, perceptions, assumptions, realities and needs are in harmony when the system is established.

- Keep testing perceptions and assumptions and use a range of communication tools to harmonize them.
- Keep checking that the process objectives align with the organization's goals.
- Use the agreed change processes to plan and execute any change.
- Determine the impact of the change on the existing processes and identify what else needs to change to maintain system integrity.
- Plan and execute the change concurrently with associated changes to documentation.
- If possible, do not remove the old routines until the new routines have been proven effective.
- Measure performance before, during and after the change.
- Do not revert to routine management until the changes have been integrated into the **culture**, i.e. people perform the new tasks without having to be told.

Tender

Meaning

A tender is a written offer to supply products or services at a stated cost.

ISO 9000 requirements and recommendations

Clause 7.2.2 of ISO 9001 requires the organization to review the requirements related to the product prior to the organization's commitment to supply a product to the customer, e.g. submission of tenders, acceptance of contracts or orders, acceptance of changes to contracts or orders.

Application

When you receive an **invitation to tender** (ITT), you should have already been selected as a capable and qualified bidder. The reason for the ITT is to establish what your organization has to offer. The customer already knows a lot about your organization, therefore, the decision that follows evaluation of a tender is to select a supplier. The fact that you receive an ITT means you are in competition with organizations that stand an equal chance of winning the contract. You may lose if your tender is not compliant, is too costly or you are unable to meet the programme requirements. However, customers are not always so methodical in their tendering process and will send ITTs, which have not been qualified, to organizations simply to obtain sufficient submissions on which to make a comparison.

Tenders are submitted only in response to a request. Other submissions are speculative and have less chance of success.

Here are ten simple rules to follow in tendering:

1 Read and understand what the customer defines as the requirements to be satisfied.
2 Clarify any requirements that may appear ambiguous, incomplete or conflicting.
3 Research the environment in which the customer operates – the constraints, politics, **critical success factors**, competition and history of the endeavour in which the customer is engaged. Ignorance of the conditions of use, what has gone before and what is critical to the customer may lead to rejection.
4 Prepare a tender that responds exactly to what the customer requires both in the structure and layout of the tender, and in technical and commercial content.

5 State the features, advantages and benefits of the chosen solution, the reasons why you consider it the best solution and what you consider is the unique selling proposition for the product or service you are offering.

6 Only promise what you can deliver. Do not overcomplicate the tender – keep it simple but do not patronize your reader. The customer has approached your organization because it believes you have the capability.

7 Cost what the customer requires, then add options for the customer to consider. Thinking that you know better is arrogant.

8 State *all* assumptions so that the customer can see the basis for your decisions. The customer will not be pleased to learn after selecting your bid and rejecting the others that you based your decisions on inaccurate information.

9 Add information that will give your tender credibility even if the customer does not ask for it.

10 Deliver the tender on time – late arrivals may be rejected no matter how good they are.

Third-party audit

A third-party **audit** is an audit performed on an organization by a person or organization that has no direct interest in its products and services – it is neither a customer nor another part of the same organization. Third-party audits are external audits.

Traceability

Meaning

Traceability is the ability to trace the history, application, use and location of an item or its characteristics through recorded identification data.

ISO 9000 requirements and recommendations

Clause 7.5.3 of ISO 9001 requires the organization to control and record the unique identification of the product where traceability is a requirement.

Application

The requirement in ISO 9001 implies that traceability applies when it is a requirement of a customer or regulator, but there are many other instances when traceability is needed:

- To isolate the root cause of a problem, remove the offending item and take corrective action.
- To determine whether all planned events have taken place.
- To locate information, product, material or equipment in order to remove, modify or update it.
- To locate organizations and personnel in order to alert them to matters of importance to them.
- To determine when and under what circumstances equipment, product, material or information was used.

With material, product and equipment, traceability is achieved by coding items and their records such that you can trace an item back to the records at any time in its life. The chain can be easily lost if an item goes outside your control. With personnel and organizations, traceability is achieved by maintaining records of their movement and contact data.

The system of traceability that you maintain should be carefully thought out so that it is economic. There is little point in maintaining an elaborate traceability system for the once in a lifetime event when you need it, unless your very survival or society's survival depends upon it.

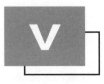

Validation

Meaning

Validation is a process for establishing whether an entity will fulfil the purpose for which it has been selected or designed.

ISO 9000 requirements and recommendations

- Clause 7.1 of ISO 9001 requires the organization to determine the required validation specific to the product.
- Clause 7.3.1 of ISO 9001 requires the organization to determine validation **appropriate** to each design and development stage during design and development planning.
- Clause 7.3.6 of ISO 9001 requires design and development validation to be performed in accordance with planned arrangements to ensure that the resulting product is capable of fulfilling the requirements for the specified or known intended use or application.
- Clause 7.3.6 of ISO 9001 requires validation to be completed prior to the delivery or implementation of the product wherever practicable.
- Clause 7.5.2 of ISO 9001 requires the organization to validate any processes for production and service provision where the resulting output cannot be verified by subsequent monitoring or measurement.
- Clause 7.5.2 of ISO 9001 requires validation of processes to demonstrate the ability of these processes to achieve planned results.
- Clause 7.6 of ISO 9001 requires measuring equipment to be calibrated or verified at specified intervals, or prior to use where necessary to ensure valid results.

Application

Validation is all about testing the validity of something: 'Will it perform the function for which it is required regardless of it meeting some pre-defined requirements?'. Validation is almost always performed on the finished article but there are occasions when validation on representative parts is more economic. Validation is normally performed once on an article and confers validity on all other articles meeting the same specification. On long production runs, verification of validation (VOV) or verification of qualification (VOQ) is performed to confirm that no changes have crept into the product that may invalidate the validation status.

When performing validation, there are three conditions that need to be met:

1 The conditions of use need to be specified in terms of function, environment, duration and user characteristics – what is it to be used for, what physical stress it will be subjected to and for how long, and what skills the people using it will need to have.

2 The article subject to validation needs to be correct itself, with no known defects, and with the right configuration meeting all requirements of its specification.

3 The validation tests need to replicate as near as possible the conditions of use.

If all the conditions are not known, the result will place a limitation on the article. If the article is substandard, the results may not be valid for other articles of the same specification.

Validation and verification

There is often confusion about the terms 'validation' and 'verification'. *Validation* has to do with the subject in question being the right subject, whereas *verification* has to do with the subject being right.

The relationship between verification and validation is illustrated in the figure.

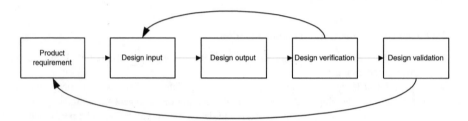

Figure 11   Verification versus validation

Some examples explain the difference (see table).

Product	Product has been verified as compliant with a particular specification but not validated for this application.
Information	The information has been verified but is not valid for this task.
Results	These results have been verified as accurate but are not valid because we need results over a different timescale.
Credit card	This card is not valid because the date has expired but the card number is verified.

Values

Meaning

In the context of management, values are the principles or beliefs that will guide the organization in fulfilling its purpose (achieving its objectives, accomplishing its **mission** and realizing its **vision**). Values are the things that are important to the organization.

ISO 9000 requirements and recommendations

Clause 5.1.1 of ISO 9004 suggests that top management should consider actions such as communicating organizational direction and values regarding quality and the quality management system.

Application

An organization adopts certain values and not others depending on its vision. Values are the key to effective management. They are at the core of every decision, every action and channel the thought processes in making decisions and taking actions – they condition the behaviour of the people in the organization and the way internal and external relationships are handled. Values characterize the culture of an organization. Values may be expressed as principles, beliefs or policies, but not all principles and policies are value statements. For an organization to be successful it needs a common set of shared values. Values should not be sacrificed to achieve an objective or accomplish a mission. Such action sends out the signal that it is OK to bend the rules. In the long term, such action becomes endemic and acts like a disease throughout the organization and leads ultimately to its downfall.

The quality management principles in ISO 9000 can be viewed as a set of values. Other values might include:

- Honesty, integrity, trust, responsibility, respect and loyalty.
- Relationships, privacy, openness, individual contribution.
- Freedom, confidentiality and financial security, life, environment and equality.
- Diversity, innovation, growth and competitiveness.

These are all positive values but there are equally negative values depending on one's point of view. Fear, tension, pressure, duplicity, uniformity, exploitation, secrecy and discrimination may be appropriate values for some organizations to fulfil their vision!

Variation

Variation is present in all systems. Nothing is absolutely stable. If you monitor the difference between the measured value and the required value of a characteristic and plot it on a horizontal timescale in the order products are produced, you would notice that there is variation over time. If you plot the values as a histogram, you would observe that there is a distribution of results around the average. As you repeat the plot for a new set of measurements of the same characteristic, you would notice that there is variation between this second set and the first. In studying the results you would observe:

- Variation in the location of the average for each plot.
- Variation in the spread of the values.
- Variation in the shape of the distribution.

There are two types of variation present: **special cause variation** and **common cause variation**. Common cause variation does not show up until all special cause variation has been eliminated.

Verification

Meaning

Verification is the act of establishing the truth or correctness of a fact, theory, statement or condition.

ISO 9000 requirements and recommendations

- Clause 7.1 of ISO 9001 requires the organization to determine the required verification specific to the product.
- Clause 7.3.1 of ISO 9001 requires the organization to determine verification **appropriate** to each design and development stage during design and development planning.
- Clause 7.3.3 of ISO 9001 requires the outputs of design and development to be provided in a form that enables verification against the design and development input.
- Clause 7.3.5 of ISO 9001 requires design and development verification to be performed in accordance with planned arrangements to ensure that the design and development outputs have satisfied the design and development input requirements.
- Clause 7.4.3 of ISO 9001 requires the organization to state the intended verification arrangements and method of product release in the purchasing information where the organization or its customer intends to perform verification at the supplier's premises.
- Clause 7.6 of ISO 9001 requires measuring equipment to be calibrated or verified at specified intervals, or prior to use, against measurement standards traceable to international or national measurement standards.
- Clause 8.3 of ISO 9001 requires nonconforming product to be subject to re-verification to demonstrate conformity to requirements when the nonconformity is corrected.

Application

Verification is about testing the correctness of something: 'Is it what it claims to be?' 'Does it meet the specification for which it has been produced?'. Unlike validation, which is performed once on a design (unless the design is changed), verification should be performed on every product that is produced to confirm that it meets the requirements. This is because there will be **variation** in materials, processes, equipment and personnel involved in its production.

There are several types of verification:

- *Verification by analysis* – confirming correctness of a characteristic by calculation or prediction.
- *Verification by similarity* – confirming correctness of a characteristic by comparison with those of other products that have been verified by other means.
- *Verification by inspection* – confirming correctness of a characteristic by examination through measurement, gauging or observation.
- *Verification by test* – confirming correctness of a characteristic by causing the product to function.
- *Verification by demonstration* – confirming correctness of a characteristic by observing its behaviour under operational conditions.
- *Verification by simulation* – confirming correctness of a characteristic by observing its behaviour under simulated conditions.

When performing verification, there are four conditions that need to be met:

1 The acceptance criteria for the article being verified needs to be specified unambiguously in terms of the physical and functional characteristics that the article is required to exhibit.
2 The specification containing these acceptance criteria needs to have been used in producing the article subject to verification.
3 The verification methods should have no effect on the characteristics being measured or any effect present should be measurable and taken into account when recording the results.

4 The **measurement uncertainty** should be known and any variation in the **measurement process** limited to common causes.

If all the conditions are not known, the result will place a limitation on the article. If the article is substandard, the results may not be valid for other articles of the same specification.

Vision

Meaning

In the context of management, a vision is an expression of what the organization wants to become, what it wants to be, to be known as or to be known for. It is the long-term view of the organization.

ISO 9000 requirements and recommendations

Clause 5.1.1 of ISO 9004 recommends that top management should consider actions such as establishing a vision, policies and strategic objectives consistent with the **purpose of the organization**.

Clause 5.3 of ISO 9004 suggests that the **quality policy** can be used for improvement provided that it is consistent with top management's vision and strategy for the organization's future.

Clause 6.2.2.2 of ISO 9004 suggests that to facilitate the involvement of people, education and training also include the vision for the future of the organization.

Application

The vision comes from the leaders – it is how they express the future for the organization. However, it must be practical and feasible while representing a challenge for the organization. The vision must also be shared by the members of the organization so that everyone clearly understands what the organization is striving to become. To create a vision for the organization top management should identify the key potential influences on the organization over the next ten years in terms of the economic, political, social and technological influences.

The vision and **mission** statements are often merged into one statement.

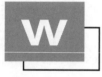

Work affecting product quality

Meaning

Quality is defined in ISO 9000 as the degree to which a set of inherent characteristics fulfils requirements. It follows, therefore, that work affecting product quality is any direct or indirect action or decision that specifies, generates, maintains, changes or verifies product characteristics.

ISO 9000 requirements and recommendations

- Clause 6.2.1 of ISO 9001 requires personnel performing work affecting product quality shall be competent on the basis of **appropriate** education, training, skills and experience.
- Clause 6.2.2 of ISO 9001 requires the organization to determine the necessary competence for personnel performing work affecting product quality.

Application

There is a note in clause 1.1 of ISO 9001 that states: 'NOTE In this International Standard, the term "product" applies only to the product intended for, or required by, a customer'. The intention of this note is to somehow limit the requirement for competence to those who impact product supplied to customers. However, there is unlikely to be any person in an organization that does not impact product quality to some degree. Leaders set the direction, and create and maintain the internal environment, which motivate those who specify, generate, maintain, change or verify product characteristics and thus impact product quality. Fail to motivate personnel and product quality will suffer.

Hence, by inserting the phrase 'work affecting product quality' in the above requirements, the authors have not placed a limitation on those who need to be competent – all personnel in an organization need to be competent if it is to satisfy its customers repeatedly.

Work environment

Meaning

The work environment is a set of conditions under which people operate. It includes **physical, social** and **psychological**, and **environmental** factors.

ISO 9000 requirements and recommendations

Clause 6.4: The organization is required to determine and manage the work environment needed to achieve conformity to product requirements.

Application

The work environment has two effects: an effect on the product, and an effect on the person. The factors of the work environment that affect the product include temperature, humidity, cleanliness, vibration and radiation. In planning the production of the product, such factors need to be taken into account. In some cases, such as in the production of food and drugs, microbiology and contamination is very important – the hygiene factors. In the production of electronic components and paint finishes, moisture and particulate cleanliness are very important.

The factors of the work environment that affect the person are physical, social and psychological. The physical factors affecting the product may have little or no effect on the person, but there are other physical factors that affect **motivation** and ability and hence the performance of the worker. (See also **physical, social** and **psychological** factors.)

Work instructions

Meaning

Work instructions define the work required in terms of who is to perform it, when it is to commence and when it is to be completed. They may also specify the standard the work has to meet and any other instructions that constrain the quality, quantity, delivery and cost of the work required.

ISO 9000 requirements and recommendations

Clause 7.5.1 of ISO 9001 requires the organization to plan and carry out production and service provision under **controlled conditions** that include the availability of work instructions.

The term 'work instructions' is not defined in ISO 9000.

Application

In simple terms, *instructions* command work to be done, **procedures** define the sequence of steps to execute the work to be done. Instructions may or may not refer to procedures that *define how an activity is performed.* In some cases an instruction might be a single command such as 'pack the goods'. *Procedures*, on the other hand, define how one should proceed to execute a task.

For example, you may issue an instruction for certain goods to be packed in a particular way on a specified date, and the package to be marked with the contents and the address to which it is to be delivered. So that the task is carried out properly you may also specify the methods of packing in a *procedure*. The procedure would not contain specific details of a particular package – this is the purpose of the instruction. The procedure is dormant until the instruction to use it is initiated or until personnel are motivated to refer to it.

ISO: Quality Systems Handbook
Fourth Edition

David Hoyle

- Comprehensive and practical guide
- Covers over 250 requirements of the standard
- Includes useful checklists, flow charts, related standards, bibliography

'With its emphasis throughout on process improvement, the book is a must for anyone in the business of implementing or interpreting ISO 9001:2000 and, more importantly, looking to gain added value and enhanced organisational performance from it.'
Quality World, May 2002

Completely revised to align with ISO 9000:2000, this handbook remains the most comprehensive book available on this series of international standards.

ISO 9000 Quality Systems Handbook is an essential guide to enable organizations to understand and apply ISO 9001:2000 requirements and the principles that underpin this radical revision of the family of standards.

Unlike other books on the subject, each element, clause and requirement is analysed in detail with practical guidance provided for its implementation.

The handbook is written for those managing existing quality systems as well as those establishing a quality system for the first time. It is written in an easy-to-follow format and style suitable for students, practitioners, discerning managers, instructors and auditors. It offers a range of solutions that are acceptable in many industries.

Based on the final draft of ISO 9001:2000, it details the differences from the 1994 version and includes check lists, questionnaires, tips for implementers, process flow charts and a glossary of terms.

CONTENTS: Introduction; Basic concepts; Origins and application of ISO 9000; General quality management systems requirements; Management responsibility; Resource management; Product realization; Measurement, analysis and improvement.

ISBN 07506445165; 688pp; 234 x 156 mm; 25 illustrations; Paperback; Oct. 2001; £30.00